MOTIVATION FOR
DREAMERS & DOERS

"It always seems impossible until it's done."

Kathryn & Ross Petras

WORKMAN PUBLISHING · NEW YORK

Library of Congress Cataloging-in-Publication Data is available.

ISBN 978-0-7611-7988-7

Workman books are available at special discounts when purchased in
bulk for premiums and sales promotions as well as for fund-raising or
educational use. Special editions or book excerpts can also be created
to specification. For details, contact the Special Sales Director at the
address below, or send an email to specialmarkets@workman.com.

Workman Publishing Company, Inc.
225 Varick Street
New York, NY 10014-4381
workman.com

WORKMAN is a registered trademark of Workman Publishing Co., Inc.

Printed in the United States of America

First printing March 2014

10 9 8 7 6 5 4 3 2 1

INTRODUCTION

"**W**hatever you can do, or dream you can, begin it."

Poet Johann Wolfgang von Goethe wrote those words hundreds of years ago, but they still have immense power today. His exhortation speaks to us across the centuries—urging us to start, to move ahead, or—to put it less elegantly—to get the lead out and get off our asses . . . now!—if we want to attain our life goals.

But what *do* we want out of life—and how in the world do we get there? If only there were some sort of magic formula for discovering and achieving our goals, something nice and neat like "optimism + hard work + determination = guaranteeing us what we want in life."

Unfortunately, life is far more complicated and difficult than that.

This is why we've collected the quotes in *"It Always Seems Impossible Until It's Done."* Sometimes we need a push. Other times we need to be reassured that failing is not the end of the world, but possibly a wonderful beginning . . . and that mistakes made may be the luckiest things that ever happened to us. Some of us may need help to figure out what it is we want to do and how we can attain that goal. Others of us may need to be reminded that it's okay to strike out on a new path. And almost all of us need a bit of motivation to stoke our fires and get our mojo back.

"It Always Seems Impossible Until It's Done" is a collection of thoughts, words, and ideas to focus or refocus on our goals, to get our confidence up to pursue those goals, and to keep the wellspring of enthusiasm and energy going as we continue our journey onward. It's a simultaneous kick in the ass, a pat on the back, and a sharing of "I did it, so can you" advice from people who have been in the same place we've been—and have done something about it. It's rappers and philosophers, social activists and presidents, poets and jazz musicians telling us to keep striving, keep going, and keep our eyes on the prize . . . just as they did.

"It Always Seems Impossible Until It's Done" makes us look at our own lives—and discover how we can do what others have already done. And just what exactly have all those rappers, philosophers, social activists, and presidents quoted in here done? *They've gotten closer to where they want to be*—a simple-sounding thing maybe, but something that most of us never do.

But we *can*.

As entrepreneur Richard Branson said, somewhat less eloquently than Johann Wolfgang von Goethe, but with unmistakable enthusiasm: "Screw it, let's do it!"

Screw it, let's do it!

—Richard Branson
entrepreneur

Hard work pays off. I am so annoyed at my father for being right about that.

—Lena Dunham
actress

MAKING MISTAKES

We have all heard the forlorn refrain: "Well, it seemed like a good idea at the time!" This phrase has come to stand for the rueful reflection of an idiot, a sign of stupidity, but in fact we should appreciate it as a pillar of wisdom. Any being, any agent, who can truly say: "Well, it seemed like a good idea at the time!" is standing on the threshold of brilliance.

—Daniel Dennett
philosopher

TO THINE OWN SELF BE TRUE

Don't bend; don't water it down; don't try to make it logical; don't edit your own soul according to the fashion. Rather, follow your most intense obsessions mercilessly.

—**Franz Kafka**
writer

GOAL SETTING: EYES ON THE PRIZE

Whatever you're thinking, think bigger.

—Tony Hsieh
entrepreneur

LESSONS LEARNED

Take a deep breath and don't take any of it too seriously.

—Cher
singer and actress

FACING FEAR

When a resolute young fellow steps up to the great bully, the world, and takes him boldly by the beard, he is often surprised to find it comes off in his hand, and that it was only tied on to scare away the timid adventurers.

—Ralph Waldo Emerson
essayist and philosopher

Doing the unrealistic is easier than doing the realistic.

—Tim Ferriss
writer

ENCOURAGEMENT

Go! Go! GO! It makes no difference where just so you go! go! go! Remember at the first opportunity go!

—Jeanette Rankin
politician

CRITICS

Honey, I am the chief of my train. If critics want to hop on board, fantastic. There's plenty of room.

—Katy Perry
singer

PREPARATION

You've got to learn your instrument. Then, you practice, practice, practice. And then, when you finally get up there on the bandstand, forget all that and just wail.

—**Charlie Parker**
musician

CONFIDENCE

Remember that a no is free. Ask for what you like, and get used to being turned down. Rejection is hard, but to get acceptance you have to put up with a lot of rejection. If you really like something, don't ever think, *Can I do this?* If you think *Can I?*, you won't. You have to say, "I'm gonna do this, and nobody's gonna stop me!" But you have to believe that, you can't just say it. It might take really a long time, because people never say you're good at first. Or if they do, you're a flash in the pan and it's over.

—John Waters
filmmaker

ACCENTUATE THE POSITIVE

I think the thing to do is to enjoy the ride while you're on it.

—Johnny Depp
actor

Whatever it is you're scared of doing, Do it.

—**Neil Gaiman**

writer

A REALISTIC OUTLOOK

The best way to make your dreams come true is to wake up.

—Muhammad Ali
boxer

NEVER GIVE UP

Courage doesn't always roar. Sometimes courage is the quiet voice at the end of the day saying, "I will try again tomorrow."

—Mary Anne Radmacher
writer

You may get
skinned knees
and elbows,
but it's worth it
if you score a
spectacular goal.

—**Mia Hamm**
soccer player

DO IT!

Don't be nervous. Work calmly, joyously, recklessly on whatever is in hand.

—Henry Miller
writer

WORKING HARD

If people knew how hard I worked to achieve my mastery, it wouldn't seem so wonderful after all.

—**Michelangelo**
artist

MAKING MISTAKES

If you don't make mistakes, you aren't really trying.

—Coleman Hawkins
musician

TO THINE OWN SELF BE TRUE

You and you alone are the only person who can live the life that writes the story that you were meant to tell. And the world needs your story because the world needs your voice.

—Kerry Washington
actress

GOAL SETTING: EYES ON THE PRIZE

The indispensable first step to getting the things you want out of life is this: decide what you want.

—Ben Stein
actor and political pundit

LESSONS LEARNED

There are no regrets in life. Just lessons.

—Jennifer Aniston
actress

FACING FEAR

The amateur believes he must first overcome his fear; then he can do his work. The professional knows that fear can never be overcome. He knows there is no such thing as a fearless warrior or a dread-free artist.

—Steven Pressfield
writer

DARING TO DREAM

Letting your mind play is the best way to solve problems.

—Bill Watterson
cartoonist

ENCOURAGEMENT

If you're going to try, go all the way. Otherwise, don't even start. This could mean losing girlfriends, wives, relatives and maybe even your mind. It could mean not eating for three or four days. It could mean freezing on a park bench. It could mean jail. It could mean derision. It could mean mockery— isolation. Isolation is the gift. All others are a test of your endurance, of how much you really want to do it. And you'll do it, despite rejection and the worst odds. And it will be better than anything else you can imagine. If you're going to try, go all the way. There is no other feeling like that. You will be alone with the gods, and the nights will flame with fire. You will ride life straight to perfect laughter. It's the only good fight there is.

—Charles Bukowski
writer

CRITICS

To avoid criticism, do nothing, say nothing, be nothing.

—Elbert Hubbard
writer

HAVING A LITTLE ATTITUDE

The Knowledge Rule 2080: From maggots to men, the world is a corner bully. Better you knuckle up and go for yours than have to bow your head and tuck your chain.

—Ta-Nehisi Coates
writer

FLEXIBILITY AND CHANGE

Everyone needs a chance to evolve.

—Jay Z
musician and businessman

TAKING RISKS

If you aren't in over your head, how do you know how tall you are?

—T. S. Eliot
writer

A REALISTIC OUTLOOK

You don't have to be
a fantastic hero to
do certain things—to
compete. You can be
just an ordinary chap,
sufficiently motivated to
reach challenging goals.
The intense effort, the
giving of everything
you've got, is a very
pleasant bonus.

—Edmund Hillary
explorer

NEVER GIVE UP

A champion is someone who gets up when he can't.

—Jack Dempsey
boxer

DO IT!

Forget past mistakes. Forget failures. Forget everything except what you're going to do now and do it.

—**Will Durant**
historian

WORKING HARD

Down time is not the name of the game.

—**Usher**

singer

MAKING MISTAKES

If you hit a wrong note, then make it right by what you play afterwards.

—**Joe Pass**
musician

Your life is precious. You've only got one. Don't waste it on bad relationships, on bad marriages, on bad jobs, on bad people. Waste it wisely on what you want to do.

—Eric Idle
actor

LESSONS LEARNED

If there is one thing that I've learned in my career, it is to do more of what's working, and less of what's not.

—Jimmy Wales
entrepreneur

COPING WITH ADVERSITY

Adversity has a way of introducing a man to himself.

—Shia LaBeouf
actor

DARING TO DREAM

Every once in a while—
often when we least
expect it—we encounter
someone more
courageous, someone
who chose to strive
for that which (to us)
seemed unrealistically
unattainable, even
elusive. And we marvel.
We swoon. We gape.
Often, we are in awe.
I think we look at these

people as lucky, when in fact luck has nothing to do with it. It is really all about the strength of their imagination; it is about how they constructed the possibilities for their life. In short, unlike me, they didn't determine what was impossible before it was even possible.

—Debbie Millman
designer

PREPARATION

You wanna climb the ladder to success and some don't appreciate the first two steps. They just wanna rush.

—**Nicki Minaj**
musician

MY BRILLIANT SUCCESS

I couldn't wait for success so I went ahead without it.

—**Jonathan Winters**
comedian

HAVING A LITTLE ATTITUDE

The only real stumbling block is fear of failure. In cooking you've got to have a what-the-hell attitude.

—**Julia Child**
chef

It doesn't matter how
far you might rise. At
some point, you are
bound to stumble.
Because if you're
constantly doing what
we do—raising
the bar—if you're
constantly pushing
yourself higher, higher,
the law of averages, not
to mention the myth

of Icarus, predicts that you will, at some point, fall. And when you do, I want you to know this, remember this: There is no such thing as failure—failure is just life trying to move us in another direction.

—Oprah Winfrey
media mogul

OUTSIDE THE COMFORT ZONE

You can become a winner only if you are willing to walk over the edge.

—Damon Runyon
writer

A REALISTIC OUTLOOK

Have no fear of perfection— you'll never reach it.

—**Salvador Dalí**
artist

NEVER GIVE UP

You must knock on doors until your knuckles bleed. Doors will slam in your face. You must pick yourself up, dust yourself off, and knock again. It's the only way to achieve your goals in life.

—Michael Uslan
film producer

ENCOURAGEMENT

To dare is to lose one's footing momentarily. Not to dare is to lose oneself.

—Søren Kierkegaard
philosopher

DO IT!

The most effective way to do it, is to do it.

—Amelia Earhart
aviator

WORKING HARD

Inspiration is for amateurs —the rest of us just show up and get to work. And the belief that things will grow out of the activity itself and that you will—through work— bump into other possibilities and kick open other doors that you would never have dreamt of if you were just sitting around looking for a great "art idea." And the belief that process, in a sense, is liberating and that you don't have to reinvent the wheel every day. Today, you know what you'll do, you could be doing what you were doing yesterday, and tomorrow you are gonna do what you did today, and at least for a certain period of time you can just work. If you hang in there, you will get somewhere.

—Chuck Close
artist

FAILING

Take risks. Ask the dumb questions. Fail if you have to, and then get up and do it again.

—Jacqueline Novogratz
entrepreneur

TO THINE OWN SELF BE TRUE

If you go to your grave without painting your masterpiece, it will not get painted. No one else can paint it.

—Gordon MacKenzie
artist

Don't work for fools. It's not worth it. Getting paid less to work for people you like and believe in is much better for you (and your career) in the long run.

—Adam Savage
special effects designer

COPING WITH ADVERSITY

The brick walls are there for a reason. The brick walls are not there to keep us out; the brick walls are there to give us a chance to show how badly we want something. Because the brick walls are there to stop the people who don't want it badly enough. They're there to stop the *other* people.

—Randy Pausch
computer scientist

DISCOVER WHAT YOU LOVE
AND LOVING WHAT YOU DO

There is no reason not to follow your heart.

—Steve Jobs
entrepreneur

Herman Melville said that artists have to take a dive, and either you hit your head on a rock and you split your skull and you die, or that blow to the head is so inspiring that you come back up and do the best work you ever did. But you have to take the dive, and you do not know what the result will be.

—Maurice Sendak
writer and artist

CRITICS

Stop letting people who do so little for you control so much of your mind, feelings, and emotions.

—**Will Smith**

actor

HAVING A LITTLE ATTITUDE

So early in life, I had learned that if you want something, you had better make some noise.

—Malcolm X
activist

ACCENTUATE THE POSITIVE

Success in life comes not from holding a good hand, but in playing a poor hand well.

—Denis Waitley
writer

OUTSIDE THE COMFORT ZONE

Go for broke. Always try and do too much. Dispense with safety nets. Take a deep breath before you begin.

—Salman Rushdie
writer

There is no such thing as a quantum leap. There is only dogged persistence—and in the end you make it look like a quantum leap.

—James Dyson
inventor

A REALISTIC OUTLOOK

To be positive at all times is to ignore all that is important, sacred, or valuable. To be negative at all times is to be threatened by ridiculousness and instant discredibility.

—Kurt Cobain
musician

NEVER GIVE UP

Whatever you do, don't stop. Just keep on going. Because one way or the other, if you want to find reasons why you shouldn't keep on, you'll find 'em. The obstacles are all there; there are a million of 'em. But if you want to do something, you do it anyway, and handle the obstacles as they come.

—Benny Goodman
musician

DO IT!

You can't be the kid standing at the top of the waterslide, overthinking it. You have to go down the chute.

—Tina Fey
comedian and writer

WORKING HARD

Allowing only ordinary ability and opportunity, we may explain success mainly by one word and that word is WORK! WORK!! WORK!!! WORK!!!! Not transient and fitful effort, but patient, enduring, honest, unremitting and indefatigable work, into which the whole heart is put. . . . There is no royal road to perfection.

—Frederick Douglass
activist

MAKING MISTAKES

Make mistakes, make mistakes, make mistakes. Just make sure they're your mistakes.

—Fiona Apple
musician

TO THINE OWN SELF BE TRUE

Be true to yourself—and keep things simple. People complicate things.

—Jay Z

musician and businessman

FACING FEAR

There's nothing wrong with fear; the only mistake is to let it stop you in your tracks.

—Twyla Tharp
choreographer

DARING TO DREAM

Go for the moon. If you don't
get it, you'll still be heading
for a star. Happiness lies
not in the mere possession
of money; it lies in the joy of
achievement, in the thrill of
the creative effort.

—Franklin D. Roosevelt
U.S. president

ENCOURAGEMENT

Power's not given to you. You have to take it.

—**Beyoncé**
entertainer

MY BRILLIANT SUCCESS

My book *The Lost Get-Back Boogie* was rejected 111 times before it was eventually published by Louisiana State University Press. When you get thoroughly rejected—and I mean thoroughly rejected— you realize you do it for the love of the work.

And you stay out of
the consequences.
I developed one rule
for myself: Never leave
a manuscript at home
more than thirty-six
hours. Everything
stays under submission.
Never accept defeat.

—James Lee Burke
writer

CONFIDENCE

Don't block your blessings. Don't let doubt stop you from getting where you want to be.

—Jennifer Hudson
actress and singer

FLEXIBILITY AND CHANGE

Real life is about reacting quickly to the opportunity at hand, not the opportunity you envisioned. Not thinking and scheming for the future, but letting it happen.

—Conan O'Brien
humorist and talk show host

There's people that say:
"It's not fair. You have all
that stuff." I wasn't born
with it. It was a horrible
process to get to this.
It took me my whole life.
If you're new at this—and
by "new at it," I mean
15 years in, or even 20—
you're just starting to get

traction. Young musicians believe they should be able to throw a band together and be famous, and anything that's in their way is unfair and evil. What are you, in your 20s, you picked up a guitar? Give it a minute.

—Louis C.K.
comedian

OUTSIDE THE COMFORT ZONE

If it gets easy, it becomes less interesting.

—Peter Jackson
filmmaker

NEVER GIVE UP

Your first 10,000 photographs are your worst.

—Henri Cartier-Bresson
photographer

DO IT!

Whatever it is—whatever it is, do it! Sure, there are going to be mistakes. Everything's not going to be perfect. I've written thousands of words that no one will ever see. I had to write them in order to get rid of them. But then I've written a lot of other stuff too. So the good stuff stays, and the old stuff goes.

—Ray Bradbury
writer

If you want to be the best, baby, you've got to work harder than anyone else.

—Sammy Davis Jr.
entertainer

FAILING

Never confuse a single defeat with a final defeat.

—F. Scott Fitzgerald
writer

TO THINE OWN SELF BE TRUE

Just keep moving forward and don't give a shit about what anybody thinks. Do what you have to do, for you.

—**Johnny Depp**
actor

GOAL SETTING: EYES ON THE PRIZE

Don't aim at success—the more you aim at it and make it a target, the more you are going to miss it. For success, like happiness, cannot be pursued; it must ensue and it only does so as the unintended side-effect of one's personal dedication to a course greater than oneself.

—Viktor Frankl
psychologist

FACING FEAR

When you learn to harness the power of your fears, it can take you places beyond your wildest dreams.

—Jimmy Iovine
music producer

DARING TO DREAM

To accomplish great things, we must not only act, but also dream.

—Anatole France
writer

PREPARATION

Think hard, always think hard, but don't worry too much about figuring out a precise strategy, a step-by-step plan. Instead, cultivate a faith, a specific faith that, by and large, doing the best you possibly can at what you value doing will bring you the chances, the opportunities you need.

—Claude M. Steele
psychologist

MY BRILLIANT SUCCESS

I used to want the words "She tried" on my tombstone. Now I want "She did it."

—**Katherine Dunham**
dancer and choreographer

HAVING A LITTLE ATTITUDE

They can't scare me, if I scare them first.

—Lady Gaga
singer

FLEXIBILITY AND CHANGE

The measure of intelligence is the ability to change.

—Albert Einstein
physicist

OUTSIDE THE COMFORT ZONE

Don't be afraid to be a fool.

—Stephen Colbert
humorist and talk show host

PERSPECTIVE

It's worth recognizing
that there is no such
thing as an overnight
success. You will do well
to cultivate the resources
in yourself that bring
you happiness outside
of success or failure.
The truth is, most of
us discover where we

are headed when we
arrive. At that time, we
turn around and say, yes,
this is obviously where
I was going all along.
It's a good idea to try to
enjoy the scenery on the
detours, because you'll
probably take a few.

—Bill Watterson
cartoonist

NEVER GIVE UP

It's hard to beat a person who never gives up.

—Babe Ruth
baseball player

DO IT!

Start a huge, foolish project, like Noah . . . it makes absolutely no difference what people think of you.

—Rumi
poet and mystic

WORKING HARD

Nothing that comes easy is worth a dime. As a matter of fact, I never saw a football player make a tackle with a smile on his face. Never.

—Woody Hayes
football coach

FAILING

I've formulated a theory: You have to continuously fail. You fail at something, then you get over it, then you fail some more. And after you fail, there's always something new there. And that something new can be really interesting. Maybe I'm not quite sure what I'm after.

—William Shatner

actor

TO THINE OWN SELF BE TRUE

You've got to listen to the voice in your gut. It is individual. It is unique. It is yours. It's called being authentic.

—Meredith Vieira
journalist

LESSONS LEARNED

How far you go in life depends on your being tender with the young, compassionate with the aged, sympathetic with the striving, and tolerant of the weak and strong. Because someday in life you will have been all of these.

—George Washington Carver
scientist

COPING WITH ADVERSITY

When adversity hits, go out and learn something.

—Julie Andrews

actress

FACING FEAR

Are you paralyzed with fear? That's a good sign. Fear is good. Like self-doubt, fear is an indicator. Fear tells us what we have to do. Remember one rule of thumb: The more scared we are of a work or calling, the more sure we can be that we have to do it.

—Steven Pressfield
writer

You can't put a limit on anything. The more you dream, the farther you get.

—Michael Phelps

swimmer

CRITICS

What you should not do,
I think, is worry about the
opinion of anyone beyond
your friends. You shouldn't
worry about prestige.
Prestige is the opinion
of the rest of the world.

—Paul Graham
computer programmer

HAVING A LITTLE ATTITUDE

Some people say I have attitude—maybe I do . . . but I think you have to. You have to believe in yourself when no one else does—that makes you a winner right there.

—Venus Williams
tennis player

FLEXIBILITY AND CHANGE

Take all the rules away. How can we live if we don't change?

—**Beyoncé**
entertainer

TAKING RISKS

Anytime I was hesitant about taking a chance, my grandmother would say, "Valerie, put yourself in the path of lightning."

—Valerie Jarrett
lawyer and political consultant

If you try to hit a grand slam, you're going to strike out.

—**Jon Stewart**
humorist and talk show host

NEVER GIVE UP

Fight one more round . . .
When your arms are so tired
that you can hardly lift your
hands to come on guard,
fight one more round. When
your nose is bleeding and
your eyes are black and you
are so tired you wish your
opponent would crack you
one on the jaw and put you to
sleep, fight one more round—
remembering that the man
who always fights one more
round is never whipped.

—James Corbett
boxer

DO IT!

I think if you do something and it turns out pretty good, then you should go do something else wonderful, not dwell on it for too long. Just figure out what's next.

—Steve Jobs
entrepreneur

Success is never so interesting as struggle—not even to the successful.

—Willa Cather
writer

FAILING

You gotta lose 'em some of the time. When you do, lose 'em right.

—**Casey Stengel**
baseball manager

TO THINE OWN SELF BE TRUE

Follow your passion.
Stay true to yourself.
Never follow anyone
else's path, unless you're
in the woods and you're
lost and you see a path.
Then by all means you
should follow that.

—Ellen DeGeneres
comedian and actress

GOAL SETTING: EYES ON THE PRIZE

Don't bother just to be better than your contemporaries or predecessors. Try to be better than yourself.

—William Faulkner
writer

Nothing is particularly hard if you divide it into small jobs.

—Henry Ford
industrialist

FACING FEAR

[The headmistress] took one look at me and said, in such a way that I have never forgotten it, "Beware of fear." It took me many years to understand the power and importance of that observation. Fear sometimes stops you from doing stupid things. But it can also stop you from doing creative or exciting or experimental things. It can cloud your judgment of others, and lead to all kinds of evil. The control and understanding of our personal fears is one of the most important undertakings of our lives.

—**Helen Mirren**
actress

DARING TO DREAM

Dream in a pragmatic way.

—Aldous Huxley
writer

MY BRILLIANT SUCCESS

I've missed more than 9,000 shots in my career. I've lost almost 300 games. Twenty-six times, I've been trusted to take the game-winning shot and missed. I've failed over and over and over again in my life. And that is why I succeed.

—Michael Jordan
basketball player

HAVING A LITTLE ATTITUDE

Hold your head high and sway your hips when you walk!

—Christina Aguilera
musician

ACCENTUATE THE POSITIVE

You may not realize it when it happens, but a kick in the teeth may be the best thing in the world for you.

—Walt Disney
entertainment entrepreneur

TAKING RISKS

Everybody knows
if you are too careful,
you are so occupied
in being careful that
you are sure to stumble
over something.

—Gertrude Stein
writer

I was once asked if a big businessman ever reached his objectives. I replied that if a man ever reached his objective, he was not a big businessman.

—**Charles M. Schwab**
businessman

NEVER GIVE UP

I am a slow walker, but I never walk back.

—Abraham Lincoln
U.S. president

DO IT!

A good plan, violently executed now, is better than a perfect plan next week.

—George S. Patton Jr.
U.S. Army general

WORKING HARD

I believe in things that are developed through hard work. I always like people who have developed long and hard, especially through introspection and a lot of dedication. I think what they arrive at is usually a much deeper and more beautiful thing than the person who seems to have that ability and fluidity from the beginning.

—Bill Evans
musician

MAKING MISTAKES

Make New Mistakes. Make glorious, amazing mistakes. Make mistakes nobody's ever made before.

—Neil Gaiman
writer

GOAL SETTING: EYES ON THE PRIZE

A goal is just a dream with a deadline.

—Drake
musician

LESSONS LEARNED

When you have a great and difficult task, something perhaps almost impossible, if you only work a little at a time, every day a little, suddenly the work will finish itself.

—Isak Dinesen
writer

COPING WITH ADVERSITY

The difference between a successful person and others is not a lack of strength, not a lack of knowledge, but rather a lack in will.

—Vince Lombardi
football coach

DARING TO DREAM

It takes a lot of courage to show your dreams to someone else.

—**Erma Bombeck**
humorist

MY BRILLIANT SUCCESS

Even as a kid in drawing class, I had real ambition. I wanted to be the best in the class, but there was always some other feller who was better, so I thought, "It can't be about being the best, it has to be about the drawing itself, what you do with it." That's kind of stuck with me. Being best is a false goal, you have to measure success on your own terms.

—Damien Hirst

artist

HAVING A LITTLE ATTITUDE

"I can't do it" never yet accomplished anything; "I will try" has performed wonders.

—George P. Burnham
writer and editor

ACCENTUATE THE POSITIVE

I am grateful for all my problems. After each one was overcome, I became stronger and more able to meet those that were still to come. I grew in all my difficulties.

—J. C. Penney
businessman

OUTSIDE THE COMFORT ZONE

Keep looking for new trouble.

—**George Clooney**
actor and director

A REALISTIC OUTLOOK

You just need to figure out what's in your control and what isn't and be okay with it.

—Santigold
musician

NEVER GIVE UP

Don't give up. There are too many nay-sayers out there who will try to discourage you. Don't listen to them. The only one who can make you give up is yourself.

—Sidney Sheldon
writer

DO IT!

The way to get started is to quit talking and begin doing.

—Walt Disney

entertainment entrepreneur

WORKING HARD

Be like a duck, my mother used to tell me. Remain calm on the surface and paddle like hell underneath.

—Michael Caine

actor

TO THINE OWN SELF BE TRUE

Do something unique that only you and no one else in the world can do.

—Robert Barry
artist

LESSONS LEARNED

The secret is keeping busy, and loving what you do.

—Lionel Hampton
musician

FACING FEAR

The word "fear" seems to
me exaggerated. Though
fear is a feeling you have
to cultivate as a creator.
Broadly speaking, I believe
that man cannot do without
fear, or being afraid.
A fearless man is, I think,
a fool, or a robot.

—Federico Fellini
filmmaker

NEVER GIVE UP

For me, I just kept going. I just kept trying. If this is not an inroad for me, I said, "That's ok, because I'm gonna find another inroad." If you can't go one way, there's many ways to get where you're going. So you just take a step back and see beyond the wall.

—Cyndi Lauper
musician

DISCOVER WHAT YOU LOVE AND LOVING WHAT YOU DO

Unless it comes unasked out of your heart and your mind and your mouth and your gut, don't do it.

—Charles Bukowski
writer

PREPARATION

Learn the rules like a pro, so you can break them like an artist.

—Pablo Picasso
artist

CONFIDENCE

When you believe you can— you can!

—Maxwell Maltz
doctor and writer

FLEXIBILITY AND CHANGE

Life is a fight. Don't let it overwhelm you. Adapt, and combat every situation it throws at you.

—Tim McIlrath
musician

OUTSIDE THE COMFORT ZONE

Somebody once said, "Everything you want in the world is just right outside your comfort zone." *Everything you could possibly want!*

—Jennifer Aniston
actress

A REALISTIC OUTLOOK

The moment you think you're somebody, you're nobody.

—Jeffrey Tambor
actor and comedian

NEVER GIVE UP

If you break your hand, try not to think about it—just go forward.

—Jake LaMotta
boxer

DO IT!

Whatever you can do, or dream you can, begin it. Boldness has genius, power and magic in it.

—Johann Wolfgang von Goethe
writer

WORKING HARD

Hold serve,Hold serve,Hold serve. Focus,Focus,Focus. Be confident,Be confident,Be confident. Hold serve. Hold,Hold,Hold. Move Up, Attack, Kill. Smile. Hold!!!

—Serena Williams
tennis player

MAKING MISTAKES

Do not fear mistakes. There are none.

—Miles Davis
musician

TO THINE OWN SELF BE TRUE

The secret is to have a sense of yourself, your real self, your unique self. And not just once in a while, or once a day, but all through the day, the week and life.

—Bill Murray
actor and comedian

GOAL SETTING: EYES ON THE PRIZE

A lot of the time our ideas
about what it would mean
to live successfully are not
our own. They're sucked
in from other people. And
we also suck in messages
from everything from the
television to advertising
to marketing. . . . We should
focus in on our ideas and
make sure that we own them,

that we're truly the authors
of our own ambitions.
Because it's bad enough
not getting what you want,
but it's even worse to have
an idea of what it is you want
and find out at the end of the
journey that it isn't, in fact,
what you wanted all along.

—Alain de Botton
philosopher

COPING WITH ADVERSITY

You're going to fall down, but the world doesn't care how many times you fall down, as long as it's one fewer than the number of times you get back up.

—Aaron Sorkin
producer and writer

**DISCOVER WHAT YOU LOVE
AND LOVING WHAT YOU DO**

A man is a success if he gets up in the morning and gets to bed at night, and in between he does what he wants to do.

—Bob Dylan
musician

PREPARATION

Our goals can only be reached through a vehicle of a plan, in which we must fervently believe, and upon which we must vigorously act. There is no other route to success.

—Pablo Picasso
artist

Never listen to criticism from anyone unless they can sign a check. Never mind what your best friend, or your aunt, or your English teacher thinks. Trust only professional criticism.

—**Marion Zimmer Bradley**
writer

CONFIDENCE

If you don't have confidence, you'll always find a way not to win.

—**Carl Lewis**
runner

FLEXIBILITY AND CHANGE

I don't control life, but I can control how I react to it.

—**Macklemore**
musician

TAKING RISKS

I've found that nothing in life is worthwhile unless you take risks. . . . Fall forward. Every failed experiment is one step closer to success. You've got to take risks. . . . You will fail at some point in your life. Accept it. You will lose. You will embarrass yourself. You will suck at something. There is no doubt about it. . . . Never be discouraged. Never— hold back. Give everything you've got. And when you fall throughout life, . . . fall forward.

—Denzel Washington
actor

NEVER GIVE UP

You're not obligated to win. You're obligated to keep trying to do the best you can every day.

—Marian Wright Edelman
activist

DO IT!

What one does is what counts. Not what one had the intention of doing.

—Pablo Picasso
artist

WORKING HARD

If you want a job, and you're not as good as the next guy, then work longer than the next guy. Work faster. Be there before him— because talented people show up late, and sometimes shit needs to get done.

—Kevin Costner
actor

FAILING

Nobody is always a winner, and anybody who says he is, is either a liar or doesn't play poker.

—Amarillo Slim
poker player

TO THINE OWN SELF BE TRUE

Do what you were born to do. You just have to trust yourself.

—Beyoncé
entertainer

So how do you know what is the right path to choose to get the result that you desire? And the honest answer is this. You won't. And accepting that greatly eases the anxiety of your life experience.

—Jon Stewart
humorist and talk show host

COPING WITH ADVERSITY

You can overcome anything if you don't bellyache.

—Bernard M. Baruch
financier

FACING FEAR

This is why we shouldn't be afraid. There are two possibilities: One is that there's more to life than the physical life, that our souls "will find an even higher place to dwell" when this life is over. If that's true, there's no reason to fear failure or death. The other possibility is that this life is all there is. And if that's true, then we have to really live it—we have to take it for everything it has and "die enormous" instead of "living dormant," as I said way back on "Can I Live." Either way, fear is a waste of time.

—Jay Z
musician and businessman

DO IT!

It always seems impossible until it's done.

—Nelson Mandela
politician and activist

DISCOVER WHAT YOU LOVE AND LOVING WHAT YOU DO

I've never worked a day in my life. I've never worked a day in my life. The joy of writing has propelled me from day to day and year to year. I want you to envy me, my joy. Get out of here tonight and say: "Am I being joyful?" And if you've got a writer's block, you can cure it this evening by stopping whatever you're writing and doing something else. You picked the wrong subject.

—Ray Bradbury
writer

PREPARATION

If I had eight hours to chop down a tree, I'd spend six hours sharpening my ax.

—**Abraham Lincoln**
U.S. president

Somebody's going to come at you, and whatever your belief, your idea, your ambition, somebody's going to question it. And unless you have first, you won't be able to answer back, you won't be able to hold your ground. You don't believe me, try taking a stand on just one leg. You need to see both sides.

—Joss Whedon
film and television producer

CONFIDENCE

I accept any challenge.

—Jennifer Hudson

singer and actress

ACCENTUATE THE POSITIVE

If you decide to run the ball,
just count on fumbling and
getting the shit knocked out
of you a lot, but never forget
how much fun it is just to be
able to run the ball!

—Jimmy Buffett
musician

TAKING RISKS

People who raise their hands deserve to be ahead of people who don't.

—50 Cent
musician

You have to finish things— that's what you learn from, you learn by finishing things.

—Neil Gaiman

writer

NEVER GIVE UP

Push yourself again and again. Don't give an inch until the final buzzer sounds.

—Larry Bird
basketball player

DO IT!

Do what you can, with what you have, where you are.

—Theodore Roosevelt
U.S. president

WORKING HARD

You practice and you get better. It's very simple.

—Philip Glass
composer

COPING WITH ADVERSITY

There is a purpose to our lives, even if it is sometimes hidden from us, and even if the biggest turning points and heartbreaks only make sense as we look back, not as we are experiencing them. So we might as well live life as if, as the poet Rumi put it, "Everything is rigged in our favor."

—Arianna Huffington
media mogul

GOAL SETTING: EYES ON THE PRIZE

If you set your goals ridiculously high and it's a failure, you will fail above everyone else's success.

—James Cameron
film producer and director

LESSONS LEARNED

Take the initiative. Go
to work, and above all
cooperate and don't hold
back on one another or
try to gain at the expense
of another. Any success in
such lopsidedness will be
increasingly short-lived.

—Buckminster Fuller
inventor

FACING FEAR

Expose yourself to your deepest fear; after that, fear has no power, and the fear of freedom shrinks and vanishes. You are free.

—Jim Morrison
musician

DARING TO DREAM

Do not confuse dreams with wishes. There is a difference. Dreams are where you visualize yourself being successful at what it's important to you to accomplish. . . . Wishes are hoping good things will happen to you. But there is no fire in your gut that causes you to put everything forth to overcome all the obstacles.

—Dolly Parton
musician

PREPARATION

It's not the will to win that matters—everyone has that. It's the will to prepare to win that matters.

—Paul "Bear" Bryant
football coach

CRITICS

If you don't have critics, you probably don't have success either.

—**Nicki Minaj**
musician

CONFIDENCE

If I am jumping into any situation, I'm thinking I am going to be successful. I am not thinking about what happens if I fail.

—Michael Jordan
basketball player

ACCENTUATE THE POSITIVE

Whether you fear it or not, disappointment will come. The beauty is that through disappointment you can gain clarity, and with clarity comes conviction and true originality.

—Conan O'Brien
humorist and talk show host

TAKING RISKS

Take a chance because you never know how perfect something can turn out.

—Wiz Khalifa

musician

OUTSIDE THE COMFORT ZONE

I keep on making what I can't do yet in order to learn to be able to do it.

—Vincent van Gogh
artist

PERSPECTIVE

For everything you have missed, you have gained something else, and for everything you gain, you lose something else.

—Ralph Waldo Emerson
essayist and philosopher

NEVER GIVE UP

Character consists of what you do on the third and fourth tries.

—James A. Michener
writer

DO IT!

There is no such thing as a long piece of work, except one that you dare not start.

—Charles Baudelaire

poet

WORKING HARD

There's few things that get you over your own crap more than working hard.

—Adam Savage
special effects designer

FAILING

I had a mother who taught me there is no such thing as failure. It is just a temporary postponement of success.

—**Buddy Ebsen**
actor

TO THINE OWN SELF BE TRUE

Your time is limited, so don't waste it living someone else's life. Don't be trapped by dogma—which is living with the results of other people's thinking. Don't let the noise of others' opinions drown out your own inner voice. And most important, have the courage to follow your heart and intuition. They somehow already know what you truly want to become. Everything else is secondary.

—Steve Jobs
entrepreneur

GOAL SETTING: EYES ON THE PRIZE

You must be single-minded. Drive for the one thing on which you have decided.

—George S. Patton Jr.
U.S. Army general

It's interesting how we often can't see the ways in which we are being strong—like, you can't be aware of what you're doing that's tough and brave at the time that you're doing it because if you knew that it was brave, then you'd be scared.

—Lena Dunham

actress

FACING FEAR

If you want to conquer fear, don't sit home and think about it. Go out and get busy.

—**Dale Carnegie**
self-help writer

DARING TO DREAM

The more you can dream, the more you can do.

—Michael Korda

editor

Keep on going, and the chances are that you will stumble on something, perhaps when you are least expecting it. I never heard of anyone ever stumbling on something sitting down.

—Charles F. Kettering
businessman

MY BRILLIANT SUCCESS

True success is figuring out your life and career so you never have to be around jerks.

—John Waters
filmmaker

CONFIDENCE

Confidence doesn't come out of nowhere. It's a result of something . . . hours and days and weeks and years of constant work and dedication.

—Roger Staubach
football player and businessman

When you're in a rut, you have to question everything except your ability to get out of it.

—Twyla Tharp
choreographer

TAKING RISKS

Do not be too timid and squeamish about your actions. All life is an experiment. The more experiments you make the better. What if they are a little coarse, and you may get your coat soiled or torn? What if you do fail, and get fairly rolled in the dirt once or twice? Up again, you shall never be so afraid of a tumble.

—Ralph Waldo Emerson
essayist and philosopher

A REALISTIC OUTLOOK

No one asked you to be happy. Get to work.

—Colette
writer

Don't believe them when they tell you how bad you are and how terrible your ideas are, but also, don't believe them when they start telling you how wonderful you are and how great your ideas are. Just believe in yourself and believe in your work and you'll do just fine.

—Michael Uslan
film producer

DO IT!

The first step towards getting somewhere is to decide that you are not going to stay where you are.

—J. P. Morgan
financier

WORKING HARD

My parents always told me, "There's always going to be someone that's better." But there's no reason why someone should outwork you. That's just an excuse.

—Derek Jeter
baseball player

MAKING MISTAKES

Anyone who has never made a mistake has never tried anything new.

—Albert Einstein
physicist

TO THINE OWN SELF BE TRUE

Someone much smarter than me once said, "Don't go with the flow. You are the flow."

—Meredith Vieira
journalist

GOAL SETTING: EYES ON THE PRIZE

If you imagine less, less will be what you undoubtedly deserve. Do what you love, and don't stop until you get what you love. Work as hard as you can, imagine immensities, don't compromise, and don't waste time. Start now. Not 20 years from now, not two weeks from now. Now.

—Debbie Millman
designer

DISCOVER WHAT YOU LOVE
AND LOVING WHAT YOU DO

You have to really believe
in what you're doing. . . .
At the end of the day, you
always have to fight for
things that are worth it.
Put your boxing gloves on.

—**Madonna**
entertainer

If I get up every day with the optimism that I have the capacity for growth, then that's success for me.

—Paula Scher
designer

CONFIDENCE

Do not let what you cannot do interfere with what you can do.

—John Wooden
basketball player and coach

ACCENTUATE THE POSITIVE

A problem is a chance for you to do your best.

—Duke Ellington
musician

OUTSIDE THE COMFORT ZONE

There's some quality you get when you're not totally comfortable. When you're not doing what you're used to, you could completely fall on your face. You could completely blow it.

—Beck
musician

A REALISTIC OUTLOOK

Work on one thing at a time until finished.

—Henry Miller
writer

NEVER GIVE UP

Champions keep playing until they get it right.

—Billie Jean King
tennis player

DO IT!

The first step to becoming is to will it.

—Mother Teresa
humanitarian

WORKING HARD

You find that you have peace of mind and can enjoy yourself, get more sleep, and rest when you know that it was a 100 percent effort that you gave—win or lose.

—Gordie Howe
hockey player

FAILING

Ninety-nine percent of all failures come from people who have a habit of making excuses.

—George Washington Carver
scientist

TO THINE OWN SELF BE TRUE

Whatever art form you're working in, it's crucial to see it clearly, to feel it clearly, and not to worry about the results, or how someone else will see it.

—Omar Epps
actor

GOAL SETTING: EYES ON THE PRIZE

I think the only reason that I'm still going now is that I don't listen. I think you can't listen. You listen to what works and what doesn't work for you and you just ignore people. Understand where it is you want to go. Then picture yourself there. If you can picture yourself there, then you can be there. Bottom line.

—Cyndi Lauper
musician

Do the big scene first, and then you can do the small scenes and have fun. It's great advice for life. I say it to my kids: Do the hard stuff first. Then you can go and do whatever you want to do.

—Bruce Willis

actor

COPING WITH ADVERSITY

Hard times ain't quit and we ain't quit.

—**Meridel Le Sueur**
writer and activist

DISCOVER WHAT YOU LOVE AND LOVING WHAT YOU DO

I've come to believe that each of us has a personal calling that's as unique as a fingerprint—and that the best way to succeed is to discover what you love and then find a way to offer it to others in the form of service, working hard, and also allowing the energy of the universe to lead you.

—Oprah Winfrey
media mogul

ENCOURAGEMENT

If you aren't going all the way, why go at all?

—Joe Namath
football player

When it takes you
20-plus years to get to
any level of success,
you're much smarter
about keeping it. There's
nothing special about
me, I just stuck with it
and worked hard.

—Louis C.K.
comedian

CONFIDENCE

I don't like to gamble, but if there's one thing I'm willing to bet on, it's myself.

—**Beyoncé**
entertainer

FLEXIBILITY AND CHANGE

Sometimes not having any idea where we're going works out better than we could possibly have imagined.

—Ann Patchett
writer

OUTSIDE THE COMFORT ZONE

You must do the thing you think you cannot do.

—Eleanor Roosevelt
humanitarian

I believe you make your day. You make your life. So much of it is all perception, and this is the form that I built for myself. I have to accept it and work within those compounds, and it's up to me.

—Brad Pitt

actor

NEVER GIVE UP

When nothing seems to help, I go look at a stonecutter hammering away at his rock, perhaps a hundred times without as much as a crack showing in it. Yet at the hundred-and-first blow it will split in two, and I know it was not the last blow that did it, but all that had gone before.

—Jacob A. Riis
social activist

DO IT!

People are always blaming circumstances for what they are. I don't believe in circumstances. The people who get on in this world are the people who get up and look for the circumstances they want, and, if they can't find them, make them.

—**George Bernard Shaw**
writer

WORKING HARD

If you can't outplay them, outwork them.

—Ben Hogan
golf player

MAKING MISTAKES

Cherish your mistakes and you won't keep making them over and over again. It's the same with heartbreaks and girls and everything else. Cherish them and they'll put some wealth in.

—Quincy Jones
music producer

GOAL SETTING: EYES ON THE PRIZE

Big goals get big results. No goals get no results or somebody else's results.

—Mark Victor Hansen
writer and speaker

If you're doing
something you've
never done before,
it's easier to feel
more relaxed about
it. When you're doing
something you have
done before, and
you can't make it any
better, then it starts
the worry.

—Ornette Coleman
musician

Look at misfortune the same way you look at success: Don't panic. Do your best and forget the consequences.

—**Walter Alston**
baseball manager

DISCOVER WHAT YOU LOVE
AND LOVING WHAT YOU DO

So, have fun. Get into your
life and do what you enjoy
and be the best at what you
can be. Maybe you won't
be successful and rich
by the world's standards,
but you will have the best
life capable of having. If
you don't do that, you're
cheating yourself.

—**Artie Shaw**
musician

ENCOURAGEMENT

Go for it, baby! Life ain't no dress rehearsal.

—attributed to Tallulah Bankhead
actress

CRITICS

Don't listen to so-called experts. I sent a tape in 1980 to all the record companies, all the majors and minors at the time, 23 of them: "Crimson and Clover," "I Love Rock 'n' Roll." They all wrote me back rejection letters. That either tells me they don't listen to the tapes they get or they can't hear hits. It's scary they passed on all of those hits. So, if you think you've got what it takes and really believe in yourself and you're ready to take a lot of crap and still want to do it, go for it.

—**Joan Jett**
musician

HAVING A LITTLE ATTITUDE

I'm not a businessman. I'm a business, man.

—Jay Z
musician and businessman

Stay fluid and roll with those changes. Life is just a big extended improvisation.

—**Jane Lynch**
actress

OUTSIDE THE COMFORT ZONE

Sometimes you just have to say, ". . . I don't know what we are doing, let's just go and see what happens." You have to embrace the experience itself, so that things you didn't intend to happen can make your work more authentic. And you have to hope that it works.

—Wayne Coyne
musician

PERSPECTIVE

Cease striving: Then there will be transformation.

—**Chuang Tzu**
philosopher

NEVER GIVE UP

My motto was always to keep swinging. Whether I was in a slump or feeling badly or having trouble off the field, the only thing to do was keep swinging.

—Hank Aaron
baseball player

DO IT!

Always bear in mind that your own resolution to succeed is more important than any one thing.

—Abraham Lincoln
U.S. president

When you get right down
to the root of the meaning
of the word "succeed," you
find that it simply means
to follow through.

—F. W. Nichol
businessman

TO THINE OWN SELF BE TRUE

Don't take advice from people like me. Do your own thing always.

—Chrissie Hynde
musician

LESSONS LEARNED

Looking back, I was very naïve about how it was going to be. In some ways my naïveté was an asset. I should've been more worried. I should've had less confidence. Because regardless of how good you are, the odds are against you.

—Corey Stoll
actor

COPING WITH ADVERSITY

When you look ahead and darkness is all you see, faith and determination will pull you through.

—Drake
musician

**DISCOVER WHAT YOU LOVE
AND LOVING WHAT YOU DO**

Do stuff you will enjoy thinking about and telling stories about for many years to come. Do stuff you will want to brag about. No one brags to the grandkids that they were one of the geniuses behind poisoning all the industrial alcohol in the country.

—Rachel Maddow
political pundit

ENCOURAGEMENT

You can't wait for inspiration. You have to go after it with a club.

—**Jack London**
writer

CRITICS

People will always find something in your work to argue with. Get used to being humbled, shutting out the noise, second-guessing yourself, and realizing that one out of six times those cretins are right.

—Lena Dunham
actress

CONFIDENCE

Believe in yourself, and go for it!

—**Emma Watson**
actress

FLEXIBILITY AND CHANGE

The secret is to move with the punch.

—**Jake LaMotta**
boxer

OUTSIDE THE COMFORT ZONE

A couple of times I've been called on to do things—jobs or whatever—where I've felt, Maybe I'm not quite ready. Maybe it's a little early for this to happen to me. But the rules are so ingrained. "Say yes, and you'll figure it out afterward" has helped me to be more adventurous. It has definitely helped me be less afraid.

—Tina Fey
comedian and writer

A REALISTIC OUTLOOK

When you've got it, you've got it. When you haven't, you begin again. All the rest is humbug.

—Édouard Manet
artist

Don't worry about things. Don't push. Just do your work and you'll survive. The important thing is to have a ball, to be joyful, to be loving, and to be explosive. Out of that comes everything and you grow.

—Ray Bradbury
writer

NEVER GIVE UP

There is no point at which you can say, "Well, I'm successful now. I might as well take a nap."

—Carrie Fisher
actress and writer

DO IT!

Knowing is not enough; we must apply. Willing is not enough; we must do.

—Johann Wolfgang von Goethe
writer

WORKING HARD

The toughest thing about success is that you've got to keep on being a success. Talent is only a starting point in business. You've got to keep working that talent.

—**Irving Berlin**
songwriter

COPING WITH ADVERSITY

The mere fact that you have obstacles to overcome is in your favor.

—Robert Collier
writer

GOAL SETTING: EYES ON THE PRIZE

Everything's in the mind. That's where it all starts. Knowing what you want is the first step toward getting it.

—Mae West
actress

Always start out with a larger pot than what you think you need.

—Julia Child
chef

DO IT!

You know what they say: "Ain't no try, ain't nothing to it but to do it."

—Bill Murray
comedian and actor

FAILING

"You have the capacity to be so much better than you are," [my drama teacher] started saying to me in September of my senior year. He was still saying it in May. On the last day of classes, he said it again, and I said, "How?" and he answered, "Dare to fail." I've been coming through on his admonition ever since.

—Aaron Sorkin
producer and writer

The ability to fantasize is the ability to survive, and the ability to fantasize is the ability to grow.

—**Ray Bradbury**
writer

I want to look back on my career and be proud of the work, and be proud that I tried everything. Yes, I want to look back and know that I was terrible at a variety of things.

—Jon Stewart
humorist and television host

HAVING A LITTLE ATTITUDE

Don't wait for them to tell you. Tell them.

— **50 Cent**
musician

Those who cannot adjust to change will be swept aside by it. Those who recognize change and react accordingly will benefit.

—Jim Rogers
financier

OUTSIDE THE COMFORT ZONE

I am always doing things
I can't do, that's how
I get to do them.

—**Pablo Picasso**
artist

A REALISTIC OUTLOOK

Nothing any good isn't hard.

—**F. Scott Fitzgerald**
writer

NEVER GIVE UP

When you're ready to quit, you're closer than you think. There's an old Chinese saying that I just love, and I believe it is so true. It goes like this: "The temptation to quit will be greatest just before you are about to succeed."

—Bob Parsons
businessman

DO IT!

As long as you can start, you are all right. The juice will come.

—Ernest Hemingway
writer

WORKING HARD

I believe in the Scottish proverb: Hard work never killed a man. Men die of boredom, psychological conflict and disease. They do not die of hard work.

—David Ogilvy
businessman

MAKING MISTAKES

The chief trick to making good mistakes is not to hide them— especially not from yourself.

—Daniel Dennett
philosopher

Whatever you do in life, aim at perfection. It will not be understood or even appreciated by most people. However, in the long run, the closer you come to achieving your own inner standards of perfection, and they'll be rising all the time, the better you'll be. In your lifetime you will come reasonably close (two or three times) to perfection. I've come about twice where I can say that is as close to perfection as I can get. I consider myself an 80-percent loser, of which I am proud.

—Artie Shaw
musician

The minute that you're not learning, I believe that you're dead.

—Jack Nicholson
actor

Obstacles don't have to stop you. If you run into a wall, don't turn around and give up. Figure out how to climb it, go through it, or work around it.

—**Michael Jordan**
basketball player

PREPARATION

Spectacular achievements are always preceded by unspectacular preparation.

—**Roger Staubach**
football player

DISCOVER WHAT YOU LOVE AND LOVING WHAT YOU DO

Whatever you like doing, do it! And keep doing it. Work hard! In the end, passion and hard work beat out natural talent. (And anyway, if you love what you do, it's not really "work" anyway.)

—Pete Docter
animator

MY BRILLIANT SUCCESS

I was never the cool kid, I was never hot in high school. I was never popular. You don't have to be perfect and you don't have to be rich and you can still be successful.

—Ke$ha
musician

CONFIDENCE

To be a great champion, you must believe you are the best. If you're not, pretend you are.

—**attributed to Muhammad Ali**
boxer

ACCENTUATE THE POSITIVE

I will not lose, for even in defeat, there's a valuable lesson learned so that evens it up for me.

—Jay Z

musician and businessman

I want to stay as close to the edge as I can without going over. Out on the edge you see all kinds of things you can't see from the center.

—Kurt Vonnegut Jr.
writer

A REALISTIC OUTLOOK

I don't wait for moods. You accomplish nothing if you do that. Your mind must know it has got to get down to work.

—Pearl S. Buck
writer

NEVER GIVE UP

Before you give up, think of the reason why you hung on so long.

—Drake
musician

DO IT!

You miss a hundred percent of the shots you don't take.

—**Wayne Gretzky**
hockey player

WORKING HARD

No masterpiece was ever created by a lazy artist.

—attributed to Salvador Dalí
artist

FAILING

If you're gonna get beat, get beat on your best pitch.

—Chris Christie
politician

If you end up with a boring, miserable life because you listened to your mom, your dad, your teacher, your priest, or some guy on TV telling you how to do your shit, then YOU DESERVE IT.

—Frank Zappa
musician

GOAL SETTING: EYES ON THE PRIZE

Never confuse motion with action.

—Ernest Hemingway
writer

LESSONS LEARNED

When I was really young,
William Burroughs
told me, ''Build a good
name. Keep your name
clean. Don't make
compromises, don't
worry about making a
bunch of money or being
successful. Be concerned
about doing good work
and making the right
choices and protect your

work. And if you build a good name, eventually that name will be its own currency. . . ." [Life] is like a roller coaster ride, it is never going to be perfect. It is going to have perfect moments and rough spots, but it's all worth it.

—Patti Smith
musician and writer

**DISCOVER WHAT YOU LOVE
AND LOVING WHAT YOU DO**

Don't become something just because someone else wants you to, or because it's easy; you won't be happy. You have to do what you really, really, really, really want to do, even if it scares the shit out of you.

—Kristen Wiig
actress and comedian

ENCOURAGEMENT

Perfection is like chasing the horizon. Keep moving.

—Neil Gaiman

writer

If you can accept losing, you can't win. If you can walk, you can run. No one is ever hurt. Hurt is in your mind.

—Vince Lombardi
football coach

ACCENTUATE THE POSITIVE

Let the bad times roll! I'm loving every minute of the struggle.

—Mary Madsen
artist

TAKING RISKS

If no one ever took risks, Michelangelo would have painted the Sistine floor.

—Neil Simon
playwright

PERSPECTIVE

Out of clutter, find simplicity. From discord, find harmony. In the middle of difficulty lies opportunity.

—Albert Einstein
physicist

NEVER GIVE UP

Just keep going. Everybody gets better if they keep at it.

—Ted Williams
baseball player

DO IT!

If you wait, all that happens is you get older.

—Larry McMurtry
writer

WORKING HARD

I hated every minute of training, but I said, "Don't quit. Suffer now and live the rest of your life as a champion."

—Muhammad Ali
boxer

FAILING

You build on failure. You use it as a stepping stone. Close the door on the past. You don't try to forget the mistakes, but you don't dwell on it. You don't let it have any of your energy, or any of your time, or any of your space.

—Johnny Cash
musician

TO THINE OWN SELF BE TRUE

You have untold strengths and resources inside. You have your glorious self.

—Sue Monk Kidd

writer

LESSONS LEARNED

I'm so sick of sarcasm and irony, I could kill! Sincerely, the real root of things is love and sacrifice. Everything else is an illusion. I'm not trying to preach here. I can't tell anybody anything. But I will say, if you're available to them, there are so many great secrets in the world, so many signs. It's when we stop for a moment and listen that the world gets interesting.

—Ben Foster

actor

COPING WITH ADVERSITY

Just keep going. No feeling is final.

—**Rainer Maria Rilke**
poet and artist

DISCOVER WHAT YOU LOVE
AND LOVING WHAT YOU DO

Your work is going to fill a large part of your life, and the only way to be truly satisfied is to do what you believe is great work. And the only way to do great work is to love what you do. If you haven't found it yet, keep looking.

Don't settle. As with all matters of the heart, you'll know when you find it. And, like any great relationship, it just gets better and better as the years roll on. So keep looking until you find it. Don't settle.

—Steve Jobs
entrepreneur

PREPARATION

The more time you spend contemplating what you should have done . . . you lose valuable time planning what you can and will do.

—Lil Wayne
musician

ENCOURAGEMENT

You can't try to do things, you must simply do things.

—Ray Bradbury
writer

CRITICS

If I had listened to the critics, I'd have died drunk in the gutter.

—**Anton Chekhov**
playwright

HAVING A LITTLE ATTITUDE

WHATEVER YOU THINK CAN'T BE DONE, SOMEBODY WILL COME ALONG & DO IT. A GENIUS IS THE ONE MOST LIKE HIMSELF.

—Thelonious Monk
musician

If you're not stubborn, you'll give up on experiments too soon. And if you're not flexible, you'll pound your head against the wall and you won't see a different solution to a problem you're trying to solve.

—Jeff Bezos
businessman

OUTSIDE THE COMFORT ZONE

Whenever you go to a different place where you feel it's just a little off-putting, that's good.

—Louis C.K.
comedian

A REALISTIC OUTLOOK

Keep your eyes on the stars, but remember to keep your feet on the ground.

—Theodore Roosevelt
U.S. president

NEVER GIVE UP

Real courage is holding
on to a still voice in your
head that says, "I must keep
going." It's that voice that
says nothing is a failure if it is
not final—that voice that says
to you, "Get out of bed. Keep
going. I will not quit."

—Cory Booker
politician

DO IT!

Get in, get out. Don't linger. Go on.

—Raymond Carver

writer

WORKING HARD

Satisfaction lies in the effort, not in the attainment. Full effort is full victory.

—Mohandas K. Gandhi
activist and Indian leader

FAILING

I waited a long time on the world before I gave myself permission to fail. Please, don't even bother asking. Don't bother telling the world you are ready. Show it. Do it.

—Peter Dinklage
actor

TO THINE OWN SELF BE TRUE

The best way to get approval is not to need it. This is equally true in art and business. And love. And sex. And just about everything else worth having.

—Hugh MacLeod
cartoonist

GOAL SETTING: EYES ON THE PRIZE

When we strive to become better than we are, everything around us becomes better, too.

—Paulo Coelho
writer

Lesson learned?
When people say, "You
really, really must" do
something, it means
you don't really have to.
No one ever says, "You
really, really must deliver
the baby during labor."
When it's true, it doesn't
need to be said.

—Tina Fey
comedian and writer

FACING FEAR

I've been absolutely terrified every moment of my life and I've never let it keep me from doing a single thing that I wanted to do.

—Georgia O'Keeffe
artist

Nothing happens unless first a dream.

—**Carl Sandburg**
poet

The moment when you first wake up in the morning is the most wonderful of the twenty-four hours. No matter how weary or dreary you may feel, you possess the certainty that, during the day that lies before you, absolutely anything may happen. And the fact that it practically always doesn't, matters not a jot. The possibility is always there.

—**Monica Baldwin**
writer

MY BRILLIANT SUCCESS

Work hard, never give up and don't fall in love with yourself.

—Martha Sturdy
artist

HAVING A LITTLE ATTITUDE

Appear tougher or cooler or funnier than you feel and there is a chance you'll make it.

—Craig Ferguson
comedian and talk show host

FLEXIBILITY AND CHANGE

I don't know where I'm going from here, but I promise it won't be boring.

—David Bowie
musician

TAKING RISKS

Take risks. Do things you can't imagine. 'Cause hey, why not, right?

—**Diane Keaton**
actress

FACING FEAR

Never let the fear of striking out get in your way.

—**Babe Ruth**
baseball player

NEVER GIVE UP

We may encounter many defeats, but we must not be defeated. It may even be necessary to encounter the defeat, so that we can know who we are. So that we can see, oh, that happened, and I rose. I did get knocked down flat in front of the whole world, and I rose. I didn't run away—I rose right where I'd been knocked down. And then that's how you get to know yourself. You say, hmm, I can get up! I have enough of life in me to make somebody jealous enough to want to knock me down. I have so much courage in me that I have the effrontery, the incredible gall to stand up. That's it.

—Maya Angelou
writer

Just because people are doing extraordinary things doesn't mean they're not ordinary people.

—**Laird Hamilton**
surfer

WHO'S QUOTED

Henry Louis "Hank" Aaron (1934–): American baseball player; major league record holder for career home runs for thirty-three years until 2007; played with the Milwaukee and Atlanta Braves, and then the Milwaukee Brewers; elected to Baseball Hall of Fame in his first year of eligibility.

Christina Aguilera (1980–): American singer, songwriter, record producer, and actress; considered one of the leading female pop stars of her time; was number 58 on *Rolling Stone*'s 100 Greatest Singers of All Time list, and named one of *Time* magazine's 100 most influential people in the world in 2013.

Muhammad Ali (1942–): American boxer; three-time world heavyweight champion; also renowned for his quick-witted repartee; one of the most recognized sports figures in history.

Walter Alston (1911–1984): American baseball player and manager; as first baseman for the St. Louis Cardinals, was in only one major league game (and struck out in his only at bat); became a player/manager for the minor league Nashua Dodgers, the first U.S. integrated baseball team since the late 1800s; as manager led the Brooklyn Dodgers to the World Series pennant in 1955, and then several more pennants after the Dodgers moved to Los Angeles.

Julie Andrews (1935–): British actress; rose to prominence as a stage actress, including starring role in *Cinderella*; later in the huge film hits *Mary Poppins* and *The Sound of Music*; has won numerous awards, including several Tonys, an Academy Award, Emmy, and Golden Globe; made a Dame of the British Empire in 2000.

Maya Angelou (1928–): American poet, memoirist, and actress; best known for multivolume memoir *I Know Why the Caged Bird Sings*.

Jennifer Aniston (1969–): American actress; best known for her role as Rachel Green in the hit television series *Friends,* for which she received a Golden Globe and an Emmy; starred in numerous films; cofounded a production company.

Fiona Apple (1977–): American singer, songwriter, and musician; her debut album *Tidal* won a Grammy for Best Female Vocal Rock Performance.

Monica Baldwin (1893–1975): British writer; niece of British prime minister Stanley Baldwin; spent twenty-eight years as a nun in an enclosed Augustinian monastery, although she felt that she "was no more fitted to be a nun than to be an acrobat."

Tallulah Bankhead (1902–1968): American actress; known for her husky voice, outrageous declamations, and unabashed lifestyle, as well as for her many roles in theater and film; most famous performances onstage were *The Little Foxes* and *The Skin of Our Teeth* and, in film, Alfred Hitchcock's *Lifeboat.*

Robert Barry (1936–): American artist; best known for his "non-material" art, producing artistic works through performance art and installations, such as his *Inert Gas Piece,* in which he opened various containers of inert gasses before groups of spectators.

Bernard M. Baruch (1870–1965): American financier, statesman, and presidential economic adviser; rose from the ranks as an office boy to a successful financier through speculation; purportedly withdrew his money from the stock market just before the big crash in 1929; later became a philanthropist.

Charles Baudelaire (1821–1867): French poet, essayist, and critic; one of France's most important poets; ushered in the era of French symbolist literature; wrote *Les Fleurs du Mal* (*The Flowers of Evil*), which highlighted the alienation and anomie brought about by industrialization.

Beck (Bek David Campbell) (1970–): American musician, singer, and songwriter; known for his experimental sound that merges many styles including folk, hip hop, soul, country, Latin, and psychedelia; considered one of the leading alternative musicians; four-time platinum artist; two albums were on *Rolling Stone*'s 500 Greatest Albums of All Time list.

Irving Berlin (Israel Isodore Baline) (1888–1989): American composer; born of Jewish parents in Belarus; had his first international hit, "Alexander's Ragtime Band," in 1911; wrote hundreds of songs, many of them huge hits, such as "Easter Parade" and "White Christmas."

Beyoncé (Beyoncé Giselle Knowles-Carter) (1981–): Singer, songwriter, and actress; burst onto the music scene as lead vocalist of the R&B group Destiny's Child; later became a top-selling soloist, known for her energetic stage performances; often writes and sings songs with a feminist theme.

Jeffrey Preston "Jeff" Bezos (1964–): American entrepreneur; founder and CEO of Amazon.com, which he created in his garage, and which is now the largest online retailer in the world; purchased the newspaper *The Washington Post.*

Larry Bird (1956–): American basketball player; spent his entire playing career with the Boston Celtics, where, as forward, he helped lead the team to three championships; was named NBA Most Valuable Player three times and made All-Star twelve times.

Erma Bombeck (1927–1996): American humorist; gained fame as a newspaper columnist writing about daily life in the suburban United States; by the 1970s, her columns were read by over 30 million readers; author of fifteen bestselling books, chiefly collections of her essays; was politically active, particularly as a backer of the Equal Rights Amendment.

Cory Booker (1969–): American politician; mayor of Newark, New Jersey; best known for his personal involvement in public service, including saving a woman from a house fire; elected junior senator in 2013, the first African American senator from New Jersey.

Alain de Botton (1969–): Swiss British writer, philosopher, and television host; his works emphasize how philosophy can help people in everyday life; best known for his bestseller *How Proust Can Change Your Life.*

David Bowie (David Rupert Jones) (1947–): British musician, producer, and actor; innovative and influential on the pop scene, he first achieved fame with the iconic hit "Space Oddity" in 1969; styles have included psychedelic, folk, glam rock (with his alter-persona Ziggy Stardust), soul, industrial, adult contemporary, and more; credited with having brought sophistication to rock music.

Ray Bradbury (1920–2012): American science-fiction writer; best known for his dystopian classic of book burning, *Farenheit 451,* as well as numerous other novels and short stories, many of which have been made into films, including the *Martian Chronicles.*

Marion Zimmer Bradley (1930–1999): American writer of fantasy novels with a feminist focus; best known for her *Darkover* series and her retake on the Arthurian legend, *Mists of Avalon,* written from the perspective of Morgan le Fay.

Richard Branson (1950–): British entrepreneur; founded the magazine *Student* as a youth; later owned a chain of record stores that became Virgin Megastores; best known for founding Virgin Atlantic Airlines; fourth richest man in the United Kingdom, knighted in 1999.

Paul William "Bear" Bryant (1913–1983): American college football player and coach; best known as the head coach of the University of Alabama football team, winning six national and thirteen conference championships.

Pearl S. Buck (1892–1973): American writer; fluent in Chinese; devoted much of her life to better East-West relations; her bestselling novel about China, *The Good Earth,* won the Pulitzer Prize; in 1938 she won the Nobel Prize in Literature; founded a charity helping Amerasian orphans.

Jimmy Buffett (1946–): American musician; famed for his so-called Margaritaville style (after his hit song that is ranked number 234 on the Recording Industry Association of America's list of "Songs of the Century"); marked by a laid-back attitude and a breezy island mentality and for his avid fan base called "parrotheads"; also a bestselling author and restaurant chain owner.

Charles Bukowski (Heinrich Karl Bukowski) (1920–1994): German-born American writer; called the "Poet Laureate of Skid Row" for his acclaimed writing on drinking, horse racing, and everyday life in a poor section of Los Angeles.

James Lee Burke (1936–): American mystery writer; best known for his series set in New Orleans with detective Dave Robicheaux; won two Edgar awards.

George P. Burnham (1814–1902): Prolific author of books ranging from *Secrets in Fowl Breeding* to *Memoirs of the United States Secret Service*; also editor of the Boston-based literary weekly *The American Union.*

Louis C.K. (Louis Szekely) (1967–): American comedian, television and screenwriter, actor, director, and producer; two-time Emmy Award winner; known for his observative, sometimes surreal, material.

Michael Caine (Maurice Micklewhite) (1933–): English actor; born in London; two-time Academy Award winner;

especially known for his distinctive Cockney accent and numerous classic roles in films such as the *Ipcress File* and *Alfie*—along with roles in numerous clunkers such as *Jaws: The Revenge,* which has now achieved cult status. Knighted in 2000.

James Cameron (1954–): Canadian director, producer, screenwriter, editor, and filmmaker; best known for his blockbusters *The Terminator, Aliens, Titanic,* and *Avatar*; winner of three Academy Awards; also a pioneer in deep-sea film documentaries.

Dale Carnegie (1888–1955): American self-help author; wrote books and developed courses in self-improvement, focusing on changing other people's behavior by changing one's behavior toward them; bestselling books include the self-help classic *How to Win Friends and Influence People* and *How to Stop Worrying and Start Living.*

Henri Cartier-Bresson (1908–2004): French photographer; called the father of modern photojournalism. He was an early user of the 35mm format; helped develop the street photography or life reportage style that was coined "The Decisive Moment," which has influenced generations of photographers who followed.

George Washington Carver (1864–1943): American scientist, botanist, educator, and inventor; born into slavery in Missouri; initially denied admission to college, finally admitted to Simpson College; best known for developing crop rotation methods to preserve nutrients in farm soil; discovered hundreds of new uses for crops such as the peanut and sweet potato, which created new markets for farmers, especially in the South.

Raymond Carver (1938–1988): American writer; widely credited with revitalizing the short story form in the United States; famous for his minimalist short stories and poems, which focused on the lives of ordinary people.

Johnny Cash (1932–2003): Singer, songwriter, and actor; known as the "Man in Black" for his dark performance clothing; country music icon who mixed hillbilly music with gospel and blues, and launched into rockabilly and rock and roll; wrote such classics as "Folsom Prison Blues" and "I Walk the Line"; the only musician inducted into the Country Music Hall of Fame, the Rock and Roll Hall of Fame, and the Nashville Songwriter's Hall of Fame.

Willa Cather (1873–1947): Pulitzer Prize–winning American novelist; best known for her depictions of pioneer life in the Great Plains, based on her own life experiences homesteading in Nebraska with her family.

Anton Chekhov (1860–1904). Russian playwright and author and physician, noted for his plays and short stories; considered one of the best short story writers ever and one of the most innovative (one of the first to break away from traditional story structure and an early user of stream of consciousness); wrote the four classic plays *The Seagull, Uncle Vanya, Three Sisters,* and *The Cherry Orchard;* in spite of his success as a writer, practiced as a doctor throughout most of his life and famously said: "Medicine is my lawful wife and literature is my mistress."

Cher (Cherilyn Sarkisian) (1946–): American singer and actress; first achieved fame as a member of the singing duo Sonny and Cher, then moved on to a solo career, performing songs that often reflected a feminist theme; became one of the bestselling singers of all time; moved on to acting on Broadway and film; among numerous other awards, won the Academy Award for Best Actress for her performance in *Moonstruck.*

Julia Child (1912–2004): American chef, food writer, and television host; served with the OSS during World War II; while in Paris with her foreign service officer husband began her culinary career at the Cordon Bleu; opened cooking school; popularized French cooking on her hit television show, which demystified cooking in a lively, enjoyable manner; wrote numerous cookbooks.

Christopher James "Chris" Christie (1962–): American politician; governor of New Jersey since 2010, known for his outsize personality and physique.

Chuang Tzu (369 BC–286 BC): Chinese Taoist philosopher more commonly known as Zhuangzi; lived a hermit's life, yet widely known for his philosophy; reportedly was offered the position of prime minister, but turned it down, saying: "I prefer the enjoyment of my own free will."

George Clooney (1961–): American actor, director, and film producer; breakthrough to popularity on hit TV medical series *ER*, then starred in major films, including *The Perfect Storm* and *Ocean's Eleven.* Voted the sexiest star of all time by *TV Guide*; winner of two Academy Awards; active in international humanitarian work.

Chuck Close (1940–): American artist; known for his hyperrealistic photorealist paintings of massive size. Although paralyzed in 1988, has continued to paint, although his mode of painting has changed—his hyperrealism is now pixelated and should be seen at a distance.

Ta-Nehisi Coates (1975–): American writer and journalist; senior editor of *The Atlantic;* writer on cultural, social, and political issues; author of *The Beautiful Struggle,* an autobiographical account of growing up in Baltimore as an African American.

Kurt Cobain (1967–1994): American musician and artist; best known as the cofounder, lead singer, and guitarist for the grunge band Nirvana, hailed as the flagship band of Generation X. Uncomfortable with celebrity, Cobain struggled with addiction; was found dead in 1994 from a self-inflicted shotgun wound to his head.

Paulo Coelho (1947–): Brazilian lyricist and novelist; best known for his book *The Alchemist,* about a boy who finds his destiny on a journey to Egypt; initially published by a small Brazilian publisher with a print run of 900 copies—it has since sold over 65 million copies.

Stephen Colbert (1964–): American satirist and comedian; host of Comedy Central's *The Colbert Report,* which satirizes conservative viewpoints; his book *I Am America (And So Can You!)* was a *New York Times* bestseller.

Ornette Coleman (1930–): American jazz musician and composer; plays saxophone, violin, and trumpet; sound is blues-based; one of the key members of the 1960s free jazz movement.

Colette (Sidonie-Gabrielle Colette) (1873–1954): French writer and performer, best known for her novel *Gigi,* which later became a famous stage and film musical; prolific author of fifty novels; called by some France's greatest female writer, particularly for her novel *Cheri,* about courtesan life.

Robert Collier (1885–1950): American writer; wrote self-help and metaphysical books focusing on visualization, confidence, and the theory of abundance; his book

The Secret of Ages, published in 1926, sold over 300,000 copies.

James J. Corbett (1866–1933): American boxer; called the father of American boxing for his studied technique: nicknamed "Gentleman Jim" Corbett for his supposed college education; best known as the heavyweight champion who defeated the great boxer John L. Sullivan.

Kevin Costner (1955–): American actor, producer, and director; known for his quiet masculine presence and low-key leading-man roles such as Eliot Ness in *The Untouchables,* Ray Kinsella in *Field of Dreams,* John J. Dunbar in *Dances with Wolves,* and Frank Farmer in *The Bodyguard.* Winner of two Academy Awards, three Golden Globe Awards, and one Emmy Award.

Wayne Coyne (1961–): American rock musician and songwriter; lead singer and guitarist for The Flaming Lips.

Salvador Dalí (Salvador Domingo Felipe Jacinto Dalí i Domènech, 1st Marqués de Dalí de Pubol) (1904–1989): Spanish surrealist painter, graphic artist, and designer; cultivated eccentricity and exhibitionism in his life and art; described his paintings as "hand-painted dream photographs."

Miles Davis (1926–1991): American jazz trumpeter, composer, arranger, and bandleader; one of the most influential musicians of the 20th century; ever innovative, he was most famous for the "Birth of Cool" sessions that revolutionized jazz.

Sammy Davis Jr. (1925–1990): American dancer, singer, and entertainer; a multitalented showman who was born in a Harlem tenement and rose to become a top entertainer and film star; a member of the famous Hollywood "Rat Pack"; a prominent civil rights supporter.

Ellen DeGeneres (1958–): American comedian, television host, and actress; began as a stand-up comedian; starred in her own sitcom, *Ellen,* and later became a successful talk show host. After coming out as gay, became a staunch advocate of LGBT rights.

Jack Dempsey (William Harrison Dempsey) (1895–1983): American boxer; known as the "Manassa Mauler"; holder of the World Heavyweight championship from 1919 until 1926; a cultural icon of the 1920s, famed for his aggressive style.

Daniel Dennett (1942–): American philosopher, writer, and scientist; his work focuses on the philosophies of the mind, science, and biology; codirector of the Center for Cognitive Studies at Tufts University; a proponent of both atheism and secularism, dubbed one of the "Four Horsemen of New Atheism."

Johnny Depp (1963–): American actor and film producer; rose to fame as a teen idol in television's *21 Jump*

Street; then moved on to roles in film, including *Edward Scissorhands* and the popular *Pirates of the Caribbean* series.

Isak Dinesen (Karen von Blixen-Finecke) (1885–1962): Danish author; most famous for *Out of Africa,* her account of living in Kenya, which gained fame as an Academy Award–winning film, as did *Babette's Feast;* also known for her macabre *Seven Gothic Tales.*

Peter Dinklage (1969–): American actor; best known as Tyrion Lannister in the HBO series *Game of Thrones.*

Walter Elias "Walt" Disney (1901–1966): American animator and film producer; best known as the creator of the iconic cartoon character Mickey Mouse; with his brother Roy founded Walt Disney Productions, which produced films, cartoons, and managed theme parks, and has become one of the largest film producers in the world.

Pete Docter (1968–): American animator, film director, voice actor, and producer; best known for directing *Monsters, Inc.* and *Up;* major collaborator with Pixar Studios, cowrote hit films *Toy Story* and *Toy Story 2;* won Academy Award for Best Animated Feature; known for emphasizing character development in animated films.

Frederick Douglass (1818–1895): American social reformer, writer, statesman, and leader of the abolitionist movement; escaped from slavery and wrote an eloquent autobiography of those early years; known especially for his dazzling oratory; first African American to be nominated for the vice presidency.

Drake (Aubrey Drake Graham) (1986–): Canadian rapper and actor; played wheelchair-bound Jimmy Brooks in teen soap *Degrassi: The Next Generation*. In 2006, began circulating mixtapes of his raps and soon signed recording deal; hit songs include "Every Girl," "Best I Ever Had," "Money to Blow," and "Take Care."

Katherine Dunham (1909–2006): American dancer and choreographer; called the "matriarch and queen mother of black dance," and "dancer Katherine the Great" by *The Washington Post*; a pioneer of African American modern dance; her dance troupe performed to great acclaim worldwide.

Lena Dunham (1986–): American filmmaker and actress; best known as the star and cocreator of the hit HBO series *Girls,* an honest look at contemporary American life.

William "Will" Durant (1885–1981): American historian; best known for his monumental eleven-volume *The Story of Civilization* and his earlier *The Story of Philosophy,* both of which were bestsellers that popularized their topic. Durant collaborated with his wife, Ariel, on these works, for which they were both awarded the Pulitzer Prize and the Presidential Medal of Freedom.

Bob Dylan (Robert Allen Zimmerman) (1941–): American musician, singer, and songwriter; rose to prominence in the 1960s with folk-rock protest songs like "Blowin' in the Wind"; his influence continued throughout the next four decades with numerous creative changes in his music and philosophy.

James Dyson (1947–): British inventor, industrial designer, and founder of the Dyson company, which makes innovative home appliances; his inventions have garnered him a fortune of over $4 billion.

Amelia Earhart (1897–disappeared 1937): American aviator and author; first female pilot to fly solo across the Atlantic; helped form The Ninety-Nines, an organization of female pilots; lost in the Pacific Ocean during an attempt to circumnavigate the globe in 1937.

Buddy Ebsen (Christian Ludolph Ebsen) (1908–2003): American actor and dancer; best known for his television roles as Jed Clampett in the hit comedy series *The Beverly Hillbillies* and as a detective in the series *Barnaby Jones*. With a career that spanned over seven decades, he began as a dancer in Vaudeville, and eventually made numerous films and television shows.

Marian Wright Edelman (1939–): American activist for the rights of children; founder of the Children's Defense Fund, which focuses on helping underprivileged, disabled, and minority children; has lobbied Congress to improve foster care, child care, and adoption; her oft-stated philosophy: "If you don't like the way the world is, you change it. You have an obligation to change it. You just do it one step at a time."

Albert Einstein (1879–1955): German-born theoretical physicist; best known for his mass–energy equivalence formula $e=mc^2$; winner of the Nobel Prize in physics; one of the most influential scientists of all time; developer of the general theory of relativity, one of the two pillars of modern physics, along with quantum mechanics. It revolutionized modern thought and the dependence on Newtonian mechanics.

Edward Kennedy "Duke" Ellington (1899–1974): American pianist, composer, and bandleader; one of the leading jazz bandleaders, with longstanding engagement at Harlem nightspot, the Cotton Club; famous for such standards such as "Sophisticated Lady" and "Mood Indigo."

Thomas Stearns "T. S." Eliot (1888–1965): Anglo American poet, critic, and editor; first book of poems, *Prufrock and Other Observations,* established his reputation; his "The Waste Land" is considered by many the most influential poetic work of the 20th century; won Nobel Prize for literature in 1948.

Ralph Waldo Emerson (1803–1882): American poet and essayist; leader of the American transcendentalist school; argued for spiritual independence, intuition, and individualism.

Omar Epps (1973–): American actor, rapper, and record producer; best known as the costar of the television series *House*; numerous film roles; heads his own production company, Brooklyn Works Films.

William John (Bill) Evans (1929–1980): American jazz pianist and composer; considered among the best jazz pianists of all time; best known for his groundbreaking trio with drummer Paul Motian and bassist Scott LaFaro in the early 1960s in the Village Vanguard sessions, which introduced a freer conception of group jazz improvisation.

William Faulkner (1897–1962): American novelist and short story writer; born in Mississippi, unsuccessful in his early years, during which he worked at a power plant; celebrated for his series of lyrical novels set in the imaginary Yoknapatawpha County in Mississippi; won the Noble Prize for Literature in 1949.

Federico Fellini (1920–1993): Italian film writer and director; began as a court reporter and cartoonist; befriended director Roberto Rossellini who helped him break into film; his first film was a flop, but undaunted, directed *I Vitelloni,* which was a huge success; then *La Strada* and a series of celebrated films, garnering four Academy Awards in the process.

Craig Ferguson (1962–): Scottish American actor, director, author, and comedian; television host of the Emmy-nominated, Peabody Award–winning *Late, Late Show with Craig Ferguson.*

Timothy (Tim) Ferriss (1977–): American writer, entrepreneur, and angel investor; best known for his books *The 4-Hour Workweek, Escape 9-5, Live Anywhere,* and *Join the New Rich,* which was a #1 *New York Times* bestseller, and named by Amazon.com as one of the top ten most highlighted books of all time.

Tina Fey (1970–): American actress, comedian, writer, and producer; broke into comedy with the Chicago troupe Second City; joined *Saturday Night Live* in 1997; acted in critically acclaimed television series *30 Rock* as well as numerous films; has won seven Emmy Awards, two Golden Globes, and five Screen Actor Guild Awards, and was the youngest-ever recipient of the Mark Twain Prize for American Humor.

50 Cent (Curtis James Jackson III) (1975–): American rapper and actor; born and raised in the tough neighborhood of South Jamaica, Queens, New York; began dealing drugs when he was twelve; launched a rapping career; was shot nine times; discovered by rapper Eminem and backed by Dr. Dre; gained prominence with his album *Get Rich or Die Tryin'* (2003), which went platinum eight times.

Carrie Fisher (1956–): American actress and writer; best known for her role as Princess Leia in the *Star Wars* trilogy; author of the autobiographical bestseller *Postcards from the Edge* and the ensuing successful screenplay.

F. Scott Fitzgerald (1896–1940): American writer; known for his novels and short stories, particularly about the so-called Lost Generation of young people in the 1920s after World War I. Widely regarded as one of the greatest American writers, particularly for his classic *The Great Gatsby*.

Henry Ford (1863–1947): American industrialist, founder of Ford Motor Company, business innovator, and promoter of the manufacturing assembly line; produced the first affordable car and, as such, changed middle-class American life; his business model was called "Fordism"—marrying mass production of goods to keep costs down with high wages for workers; was one of the richest people in the world, left most of his fortune to Ford Foundation; was also noted for his pascifism during World War I and his anti-semitic beliefs.

Benjamin A. (Ben) Foster (1980–): American actor; dropped out of high school and moved to Los Angeles to pursue an acting career; best known role as the killer Charlie Prince in *3:10 to Yuma*.

Anatole France (1844–1924): French writer; began his career as a journalist and poet, wrote several bestselling novels, including *Thaïs,* about a courtesan in ancient Alexandria, and the satirical *Penguin Island;* awarded the Nobel Prize for Literature in 1921.

Viktor Frankl (1905–1997): Austrian psychiatrist; as a Jew was sent to Nazi death camps including Auschwitz; out of this experience developed his theory of logotherapy—human motivation comes from a "will to meaning." After World War II, became head of neurology at Vienna Polyclinic Hospital; an avid mountain climber and pilot.

Buckminster Fuller (1895–1983): American independent inventor and futurist who practiced what he preached—a dynamic lifestyle of invention and popularizing his ideas of efficient living through his personally modified systems analysis; invented the geodesic dome among numerous other innovations.

Lady Gaga (Stefani Germanotta) (1986–): American singer/activist, known for her flamboyant style, outrageous fashions, and arty sensibility; rose to fame in 2008 with her debut album, which was followed the following year by a chart-breaking extended play *The Fame Monster* and its Monster Ball tour, which was one of the highest grossing tours of all time; closely involved with her rabid fan base called "little monsters"; has won five Grammy Awards and thirteen MTV Video Music Awards.

Neil Gaiman (1960–): English author; broad range of works from short stories to graphic novels to screenplays; most famous for his Sandman series, the first comic book to ever win a literary award.

Mohandas K. Gandhi (1869–1948): Indian spiritual and political leader; known as Mahatma (Great Soul). Pioneered nonviolent resistance; regarded as a great politician and moral leader; even his enemies conceded his personal honesty and integrity; led nonviolent civil disobedience movement against British rule in India; was assassinated in 1948 by a Hindu fanatic.

Philip Glass (1937–): American composer; one of the most influential composers of the later 20th century, his modern form of music has been termed "minimalism." Glass prefers to call his form "music with repetitive structures," and more recently "classicist," in the style of Bach and Schubert.

Johann Wolfgang von Goethe (1749–1832): German poet, playwright, politician, and artist; considered the greatest writer of the German romantic period; a worldwide success at age twenty-five for his monologue novel *The Sorrows of Young Werther;* best known for his two-part poetic drama *Faust,* which he started around the age of twenty-three and didn't finish until shortly before his death sixty years later.

Benjamin David "Benny" Goodman (1909–1986): American clarinetist and bandleader; known as the "King of Swing"; created many jazz swing hits; in 1936 had fifteen top 10 hits; led the first jazz orchestra to play at Carnegie Hall; famous also for leading one of the first racially integrated bands.

Paul Graham (1964–): British computer programmer, entrepreneur, and writer; best known for creating the innovative programming language LISP and an entrepreneurial seed capital firm for computer start-ups.

Wayne Gretzky (1961–): Canadian ice hockey player and coach; nicknamed "the Great One"; is the leading scorer in National Hockey League history; often called the greatest hockey player ever; among numerous awards, five Hart trophies as most valuable player and five Lady Byng trophies for sportsmanship; has spoken out against fighting in the sport.

Laird Hamilton (1964–): American surfer; best known for his big-wave surfing, regularly surfs swells of thirty-five feet and as high as seventy feet; coinventor of "tow-in" surfing; renowned as the world's best surfer; particularly famous for riding a huge and dangerous wave at Tahiti's Teahupo'o break.

Mia Hamm (1972–): American soccer player; played forward for the U.S. women's national soccer team; scored 158 international goals, more than any other soccer player in world play; founded a professional women's soccer team.

Lionel Hampton (1908–2002): American jazz musician; known especially for being one of the first and best jazz vibraphone players; worked with jazz great Benny Goodman; later formed his own iconic big band, The Lionel Hampton Orchestra.

Mark Victor Hansen (1948–): American motivational speaker; best known for being a cofounder and creator of the inspirational Chicken Soup for the Soul book series.

Coleman Hawkins (1904–1969): American jazz musician; one of the first major jazz tenor saxophonists; nicknamed "Hawk" and "Bean"; hugely influential in swing and big band music; helped develop bebop. Miles Davis once said: "When I heard Hawk, I learned to play ballads."

Wayne Woodrow "Woody" Hayes (1913–1987): American football player and coach; best known for leading the Ohio State Buckeyes to five national and thirteen Big Ten championships; known for the conservative "crunching muscle against muscle" football style (using little passing) and for being among the first coaches to recruit African American players and assistant coaches.

Ernest Hemingway (1899–1961): American writer; known for his terse writing style; won the Pulitzer Prize in 1953 for *The Old Man and the Sea* and the Nobel Prize in Literature in 1954.

Kenneth Hildebrand: American writer; author of inspirational books such as *Achieving Real Happiness* and *Finding Real Happiness.*

Edmund Hillary (1919–2008): New Zealand mountaineer, philanthropist, explorer; best known as being one of the two first men to reach the peak of Mount Everest (along with Tenzing Norgay); also reached the North and South Poles; devoted much of his life to helping the Sherpa people of Nepal.

Damien Hirst (1965–): British artist and entrepreneur; reportedly Britain's richest artist; a leader of the YBAs (Young British Artists); best known for a series of works that involved exhibiting preserved animals in tanks.

Ben Hogan (1912–1997): American golfer; nine career championships, one of only five players to win the Masters Tournament, the British Open, the U.S. Open, and the PGA Championship; famed for golf swing theory and ball striking ability; considered one of the world's greatest golfers.

Gordon "Gordie" Howe (1928–): Canadian ice hockey player; known by the trademarked name "Mr. Hockey" and regarded as one of the NHL's greatest all-time players. As a player for the Detroit Red Wings, he led them to four Stanley Cups and seven first-place finishes in regular season play, a feat never equaled in NHL history.

Tony Hsieh (1973–): American businessman and entrepreneur; best known as founder of online shoe and clothing retailer Zappos.com; a pioneer in business uses for Twitter.

Elbert Hubbard (1856–1915): American writer, artist, philosopher, and publisher; founded the famous Arts and Crafts movement artisan community of Roycroft; published books and magazines expounding his anarchist, socialist, antiwar, and artistic views; died as a passenger on the torpedoed *Lusitania* in 1915.

Jennifer Hudson (1981–): American singer and actress; was seventh-place finalist on *American Idol* in 2004; two years later, appeared in *Dreamgirls,* for which she won five major awards, including a Best Supporting Actress Academy Award; faced with personal tragedy when her mother, brother, and nephew were murdered; has since resumed her career doing numerous personal appearances and serving as spokeswoman for Weight Watchers.

Arianna Huffington (née Stassinopoulous) (1950–): Greek-American writer, columnist, media entrepreneur; founder of news website *The Huffington Post;* seesawed between political ideologies—was first a liberal Democrat, then a conservative pundit and wife of Republican congressman Michael Huffington, then switched back to liberalism; considered one of the most influential media leaders.

Aldous Huxley (1894–1963): English writer, essayist, and novelist; most famous work, *Brave New World,* explored the concept of a dehumanized future; heavily involved in pacifism and humanism; also noted for his experimentation with psychedelic drugs.

Chrissie Hynde (1951–): American singer, songwriter, and musician; best known as the leader of the rock/new wave band The Pretenders; also a prominent animal-rights activist and vegan.

Eric Idle (1943–): English actor, comedian, writer, and composer; member of the famous comedy troupe Monty Python; cowrote and appeared in popular Python films, including *Life of Brian* and *Monty Python and the Holy Grail;* converted the latter into the highly successful Broadway musical *Spamalot.*

James "Jimmy" Iovine (1953–): American music producer and entertainment entrepreneur; cofounded Interscope Records, which became Interscope Geffen A&M after a

1999 merger; produced films starring rappers including Eminem's *8 Mile*; cofounded headset company Beats by Dr. Dre and worked with that company to develop digital music service; received honorary Grammy Award for his work; mentor on *American Idol*.

Peter Jackson (1961–): New Zealand film director, producer, and screenwriter; best known for his adaptation of J.R.R. Tolkien's *Lord of the Rings* trilogy; interested in filmmaking as a child, attempted to remake *King Kong* when he was just twelve years old; began as director of horror comedies; won Academy Award for Best Director in 2003.

Valerie Jarrett (1956–): Iranian-born American lawyer and presidential adviser; senior adviser to President Obama; prominent Chicago lawyer and businesswoman; was co-chairperson of the Obama-Biden Transition Project before being appointed Assistant to the President for Public Engagement and Intergovernmental Affairs.

Jay Z (Shawn Carter) (1969–): American rapper/hip hop artist, producer, and entrepreneur; considered one of the most influential hip hop artists of all time and one of the most successful artists of the 2000s, has won 17 Grammy Awards and has sold over 75 million records worldwide; as a businessman, is cocreator of Rocawear clothing line, founder of Roc Nation Sports Agency, and owner of the nightclub 40/40 Club. Married to entertainer Beyoncé Knowles.

Derek Jeter (1974–): American baseball player; spent eighteen seasons as shortstop with the New York Yankees; regarded as central to the Yankees success, helping lead them to five World Series championships; known as "Captain Clutch" and "Mr. November" for his role in leading the Yankees in tough postseason play.

Joan Jett (1958–): American rock guitarist, singer, and songwriter; called the Queen of Rock 'n' Roll, especially for her part in the band Joan Jett and the Blackhearts and their hit single, "I Love Rock 'n' Roll," along with other hits, including "Crimson and Clover."

Steve Jobs (1955–2011): American entrepreneur, inventor, and computer innovator, called "the Father of the Digital Revolution"; cofounder of the iconic Apple Inc., and greatly responsible for the growth of the personal computer market; also cofounded Pixar Animation Studios and served on the board of Walt Disney. Left Apple in 1985 to found computer company NeXT and returned to Apple in 1998 after Apple floundered in the marketplace; his later years at Apple saw the introduction of the iMac, iPod, iPad, iPhone, and iTunes.

Quincy Jones (1933–): American record producer, arranger, and composer; began as a trumpet player for Lionel Hampton, then arranged songs for such

greats as Count Basie; became musical director for
Dizzy Gillespie and later for Mercury Records; wrote
numerous scores for such hit shows as *Sanford and
Son* and numerous films; formed his own music label;
produced Michael Jackson hits, including *Thriller.*

Michael Jordan (1963–): American basketball player;
considered by many to be the greatest basketball
player of all time; winner of numerous awards,
including five MVP awards, ten All-NBA First Team
designations, nine All-Defensive First Team honors;
retired to play professional baseball, then returned to
win more championships; also known as one of the
most successful sports marketers and promoters.

Franz Kafka (1883–1924): German-speaking Jewish writer
who lived in Prague, at the time part of the Austro-
Hungarian Empire; one of the most influential writers
of the 20th century whose stories and novels, including
The Metamorphosis and *The Trial,* explore existentialist
themes of absurdity, alienation, despair, and mystical
transformations. The term "Kafkaesque" has entered
English to describe the surreal themes he wrote about.

Diane Keaton (Diane Hall) (1946–): American actress,
director, producer, and screenwriter; first hit the big
screen in 1970 as Michael Corleone's wife Kay in *The
Godfather,* perhaps best known for her work with
Woody Allen; appeared in eight of his films between

1971 and 1993, including her iconic role in *Annie Hall,* which won her the Academy Award for Best Actress; has continued to act in major films both in dramatic and comedic roles.

Ke$ha (Kesha Rose Sebert) (1987–): American rapper, singer, and songwriter; signed to a record label in 2005 at age eighteen; her big break came after appearing on rapper Flo Rida's hit single "Right Round" in 2009; her first album, *Animal,* debuted at number one in the United States. Her trademark "talky" rap technique, yodeling, and auto-tune have propelled her to many top 10 hits.

Charles F. Kettering (1876–1958): American inventor, engineer, and businessman; holder of 186 patents; invented the electrical starting motor, leaded gasoline, the first aerial missile, and in association with Dupont, Freon refrigerant and Duco lacquer, the first practical colored paints for cars. Helped revolutionize the locomotive and heavy equipment industries with his advancing the two-stroke diesel engine.

Wiz Khalifa (Cameron Jibril Thomaz) (1987–): American rapper and songwriter; released debut album *Show and Prove* in 2006; his album *Rolling Papers* made number two on *Billboard*; voted best new artist at the BET awards in 2011.

Sue Monk Kidd (1948–): American writer; best known for her first novel, *The Secret Life of Bees*; also known for her works on contemplative Christianity and feminism.

Søren Kierkegaard (1813–1855): Danish philosopher and theologian; considered the first existentialist philosopher, especially in the Absurdist tradition, and an important Christian thinker; complex works emphasize religious themes and personal choices in life; considered a cross-disciplinary thinker combining elements of philosophy, theology, psychology, and literature.

Billie Jean King (1943–): American tennis player; ranked as the world's number-one professional tennis player in the 1960s and '70s; won thirty-nine grand slam titles; founded Women's Tennis Association; a strong feminist advocate; one of the first major sports figures to come out as gay, for which she lost numerous business endorsements and was forced to return to competitive tennis.

Michael Korda (1933–): American editor and writer; rose to become editor in chief of major publisher Simon & Schuster; edited many high-profile writers, including William L. Shirer; has written several books, both fiction and nonfiction, including two about his famous family, which included director Alexander Korda.

Shia LaBeouf (1986–): American actor; made his film debut in *Holes* in 2003; moved on to become a leading man in films including *Transformers, Indiana Jones and the Kingdom of the Crystal Skull,* and *Wall Street: Money Never Sleeps.*

Giacobbe "Jake" LaMotta (1921–): American boxer; nicknamed the "The Bronx Bull" and "The Raging Bull"; former World Middleweight Champion; his autobiography, *Raging Bull: My Story,* inspired the classic Oscar-winning film directed by Martin Scorsese; the lead actor, Robert De Niro, trained with LaMotta until he had the moves of a professional boxer.

Cyndi Lauper (1953–): American singer, songwriter, and actress; one of the biggest stars of the early MTV era, with continued musical success into the 2010s; her latest work, the Broadway musical *Kinky Boots,* won her a Tony Award.

Meridel Le Sueur (1900–1996): American writer and journalist; her writing, both fiction and nonfiction, focused on the suffering of the working class, especially women; distinctive lyrical style won her numerous readers; blacklisted in the McCarthy era but still lectured and wrote; during the 1960s participated in campus protests; active in progressive causes until her death at age ninety-six.

Carl Lewis (1961–): American track and field star; sprinter and long jumper; winner of ten Olympic medals, nine of them gold; named Sportsman of the Century by the International Olympic Committee and Olympian of the Century by *Sports Illustrated.*

Lil Wayne (Dwayne Michael Carter Jr.) (1982–): American rapper; born in New Orleans, began career at age nine with the BG'z; joined New Orlean's Hot Boys; debut solo album was certified platinum soon after release; dubbed himself greatest rapper alive on his 2005 album *Tha Carter II,* which was followed by a period of intense creativity; in 2012 passed Elvis Presley as the artist with the most entries on the *Billboard* Hot 100.

Abraham Lincoln (1809–1865): American statesman; 16th president of the United States; president during the Civil War; championed the Union and emancipation for slaves, modernized the economy, and strengthened the federal government; widely considered one of the three greatest U.S. presidents; assassinated while still in office.

Vincent Thomas "Vince" Lombardi (1913–1970): American football coach; spent nine years as head coach of the Green Bay Packers, leading them to five NFL championships; known for his inspiring pep talks and go-get-'em demeanor.

Jack London (1876–1916): American writer, journalist, and social activist; best known for his Klondike Gold Rush–era novels *Call of the Wild* and *White Fang;* one of the first writers to achieve wealth as a writer of fiction.

Jane Lynch (1960–): American actress, singer, and comedian; has won numerous awards for her roles in television and film, including an Emmy, Golden Globe, and People's Choice for favorite television comedy actress; best known for her role in television's *Glee*.

Gordon MacKenzie: Canadian artist, teacher, and author; best known for his watercolors; work focuses on nature, "the ultimate teacher" as he terms it.

Macklemore (Ben Haggerty) (1983–): American rapper; born in Seattle; started writing his own lyrics at age fourteen; after several solo productions teamed up with producer Ryan Lewis; their single "Thrift Shop" reached number one on the *Billboard* Top 100 chart, one of only two singles not produced by a major label to do so; an unconventional lyrical rapper; gives an annual pizza party for his fans.

Hugh MacLeod: American cartoonist and marketing pioneer; creator of innovative "cube grenades," targeted cartoons to inspire businesses to innovatively increase their business; active in web strategies for businesses.

Madonna (Madonna Louise Ciccone) (1958–): American entertainer, bestselling female recording artist of all time (according to Guinness World Records) with over 300 million record sales worldwide; gained fame in 1983 with her debut album *Madonna* as well as her downtown look, which was emulated by millions of young women; has since had a string of successful albums including two Grammy Award winners, numerous chart-topping singles, and a somewhat spotty acting career. Is both praised and criticized for reinventing her onstage persona and for the elaborate production values of her live shows.

Rachel Maddow (1973–): American radio and television political commentator and host; known for her outspoken liberal views, stating, "I'm undoubtedly a liberal, which means that I'm in almost total agreement with the Eisenhower-era Republican party platform"; the first openly gay major news anchor.

Mary Madsen: American artist; Utah native who moved to Albuquerque; work revolves around Southwestern themes.

Malcolm X (Malcolm Little; El-Hajj Malik El-Shabazz) (1925– 1965): American minister and human-rights activist; leader of the civil rights movement in the 1950s and '60s; charismatic but controversial, he eschewed nonviolent action but advocated a stronger response to white supremacy; spokesman for the Nation of Islam, which he left in 1964 to form his own group, the Muslim Mosque; assassinated less than a year later by three Nation of Islam members.

Maxwell Maltz (1889–1975): American cosmetic surgeon and self-help pioneer; his bestselling book on positive self-image, *Psycho-Cybernetics,* advocated that people obtain a clear vision of themselves before setting their goals, otherwise they get trapped by self-limiting beliefs.

Nelson Mandela (1918–2013): South African politician and activist; anti-apartheid revolutionary who spearheaded a campaign against the South African government; imprisoned by the apartheid separatist government for twenty-seven years; was awarded Nobel Peace Prize in 1993 (with president F. W. de Klerk) for their joint efforts against racism. Became the first black president of South Africa (1994–1999); celebrated for his program of national reconciliation between whites and blacks.

Édouard Manet (1832–1883): French artist; a major painter in the transition from Realism to Impressionism; he broke with traditional techniques of representation and chose contemporary subjects. His famous *Le déjeuner sur l'herbe (The Luncheon on the Grass)* was panned by critics, but it was the prime inspiration of young artists who later would found the Impressionist movement.

Timothy James "Tim" McIlrath (1978–): American musician; lead singer, rhythm guitarist, songwriter, and cofounder of the punk rock band Rise Against; avid supporter and promoter of animal rights group PETA.

Larry McMurtry (1936–): American novelist, screenwriter, and bookseller; best known for his works set in Texas or the Old West, especially his Pulitzer prize–winning novel, *Terms of Endearment,* and *Lonesome Dove,* which became an acclaimed television miniseries. A lifelong bookseller, his Archer City, Texas, bookstore was one of the largest bookstores in the United States.

Michelangelo (Michelangelo di Lodovico Buonarroti Simoni) (1475–1564): Italian painter, sculptor, architect, and poet; considered one of the greatest artists of the Italian Renaissance; created such sculptural masterpieces as the 18-foot-high *David* and the *Pietà,* along with his famous Sistine Chapel ceiling painting and *The Last Judgment.* He had a reputation for being prickly tempered, mistrusting, and lonely—and an artistic genius.

James A. Michener (1907–1997): American writer; wrote over forty books, chiefly highly researched historical sagas; won a Pulitzer in Fiction for his *Tales of the South Pacific* (which inspired the musical *South Pacific*); other famous works include *Hawaii, Centennial, Chesapeake,* and *Caribbean.*

Henry Miller (1891–1980): American writer; best known for his semiautobiographical novels *Tropic of Cancer* and *Tropic of Capricorn* (banned from the United States until 1961 for their purported obscenity); a literary innovator who mixed actual and imagined experiences; he pushed against legal and social restrictions.

Debbie Millman: American graphic designer; also known for her work as a brand consultant, writer, and educator; host of podcast *Design Matters*; work is characterized by hand-drawn typography.

Nicki Minaj (Onika Tanya Maraj) (1982–): American hip-hop artist, actress, and *American Idol* host; born in

Trinidad; famous for her fast-paced rapping technique with use of alter egos and accents; garnered numerous awards and chart-topping sales. Also known for her colorful wigs and eccentric fashions.

Helen Mirren (Ilyena Mironoff) (1945–): British actress; winner of multiple acting awards, including an Oscar, three Golden Globes, and four Emmys. Received a damehood from Queen Elizabeth in 2003.

Thelonious Monk (1917–1982): American jazz pianist and composer; noted for his improvisational style, which was marked by dissonance and unorthodox melodies; composed about seventy songs, including such jazz standards as "Round Midnight" and "Straight No Chaser." He has become the second-most recorded jazz composer.

John Pierpont (J. P.) Morgan (1837–1913): American financier; the son of a banker, worked for his father, then formed his own banking company, which bore his name; became the most powerful financier in the United States; the U.S. government turned to him to help in the Panic of 1893; created railroad and steel monopolies; used his wealth to create huge collections of art and books, which he endowed to the Metropolitan Museum of Art and The Morgan Library and Museum, both in New York.

James Douglas "Jim" Morrison (1943–1971): American rocker and poet; lead singer and songwriter for the iconic 1960s rock group The Doors; considered one of the most compelling rock performers in music history; included on *Rolling Stone*'s 100 Greatest Singers of All Time list; his lyrics and poetry were heavily surrealistic and allegorical; called himself the "King of Orgasmic Rock"; died of an alleged heroin overdose at age twenty-seven.

William James "Bill" Murray (1950–): American actor and comedian; first gained fame on the hit comedy show *Saturday Night Live,* for which he won an Emmy; went on to star in several hit comedy films, including *Ghostbusters* and *Groundhog Day*; later moved into drama, garnering an Academy Award nomination for Best Actor for his role in *Lost in Translation.*

Joseph "Joe" Namath (1943–): American football player; quarterback with the New York Jets and later the Los Angeles Rams; famous for successfully predicting the Jets' victory in Super Bowl III.

F. W. Nichol (1892–1955): American businessman; vice president and general manager of IBM; served on New York University Governing Council.

John Joseph "Jack" Nicholson (1937–): American actor, director, producer, and writer; a screen icon, beginning with his breakthrough role in the countercultural classic *Easy Rider*; seminal roles in *Five Easy Pieces, Chinatown, One Flew Over the Cuckoo's Nest,* and *Terms of Endearment*; has won numerous awards, including three Academy Awards.

Jacqueline Novogratz: American financial and social entrepreneur; after working as an international banker turned her focus on helping the needy; founded The Philanthropy Workshop and The Next Generation Leadership programs at the Rockefeller Foundation; in 2001 founded the nonprofit venture capital Acumen Fund to help combat poverty around the world; has invested over $50 million in fifty different businesses.

Conan O'Brien (1963–): American comedian and television host; known for his awkward, self-deprecating humor; began career writing for comedy shows, moved to *Saturday Night Live*; became host of his own very popular talk/comedy shows, the most recent of which, *Conan,* airs on TBS.

David Ogilvy (1911–1999): English advertising executive; often called "The Father of Advertising" for his innovative and hard-charging style; famed for clever copy such as his "At sixty miles an hour, the loudest noise in this new Rolls-Royce comes from the electric clock."

Georgia O'Keeffe (1887–1986): American artist; renowned for her portrayal of the essential abstract forms in nature, especially landscapes, bones, and flowers; her budlike, erotic flowers are particularly famous.

Charles "Charlie" Parker Jr. (1920–1955): American jazz saxophonist and composer; known as "Yardbird" and "Bird"; renowned especially for his jazz innovations, including rapid passing chords, new variants of altered chords, and chord substitutions. Miles Davis once said, "You can tell the history of jazz in four words: Louis Armstrong. Charlie Parker."

Robert "Bob" Parsons (1950–): American entrepreneur; born to a poor family in inner-city Baltimore; graduated magna cum laude from University of Baltimore; as a self-taught programmer founded an accounting technology company, then GoDaddy, a major Internet domain and web hosting company.

Dolly Parton (1946–): American singer, songwriter, and actress; one of the most prominent country singers of all time, with over $100 million in record sales; hit songs include "I Will Always Love You" and "Jolene"; has over twenty-five gold and platinum albums; many of her songs reflect her humble country and evangelical background.

Joe Pass (Joseph Anthony Jacobi Passalacqua) (1929–1994): American musician; one of the greatest jazz guitarists of the 20th century; began playing professionally at age fourteen; his innovative style involving chord inversions and progressions continues to influence modern guitarists.

Ann Patchett (1963–): American author; winner of the PEN/Faulkner award for her novel *Bel Canto,* about the complicated relationship between hostages and terrorists.

George S. Patton Jr. (1885–1945): U.S. Army general; best known for his hard-charging command of the Seventh U.S. Army and the Third U.S. Army in the European Theater during World War II. Leading from the front lines, his ideas of rapid, aggressive warfare were adopted by the U.S. officer corps.

Randolph "Randy" Pausch (1960–2008): American computer science professor, best known for his "The Last Lecture: Really Achieving Your Childhood Dreams" at Carnegie Mellon, about the wisdom he wished to impart after receiving a terminal diagnosis of pancreatic cancer. The lecture later became the source of a bestselling book.

James Cash (J. C.) Penney (1875–1971): American businessman; worked at a dry-goods store as a young man; opened his own store in 1902; expanded it into a chain of 175 stores by the time he retired in 1912; stayed on the company Board of Directors until his death in 1971.

Katy Perry (Katheryn Elizabeth Hudson) (1984–): American pop singer and songwriter; began in her teen years as a gospel singer; gained fame with her second mainstream studio album *One of the Boys*; has garnered five number-one hits on the *Billboard* Hot 100.

Michael Phelps (1985–): American swimmer; most decorated Olympic athlete of all time with twenty-two medals, including eighteen gold.

Pablo Picasso (1881–1973): Spanish painter and sculptor; famed for his artistic innovation and versatility as well as for the beauty of his creations. *Guernica* is one of his Cubist masterpieces, a style he pioneered.

William Bradley "Brad" Pitt (1963–): American actor and film producer; known for numerous roles in major films, beginning with *Thelma and Louise,* the cult film *Fight Club,* and many other hits, including *Legends of the Fall, Troy,* and *Mr. and Mrs. Smith*; he was nominated for four Academy Awards; active in social issues domestically and internationally.

Steven Pressfield (1943–): American author; his first book, *The Legend of Bagger Vance,* was published when the author was in his fifties and was made into a film by Robert Redford. His next book, *Gates of Fire,* was about the Spartans at Thermopylae and is part of the curriculum at several U.S. military schools.

Mary Anne Radmacher: American writer, artist, and "actionista," who, as she says, has been providing inspiration to the world for over thirty years; author of such bestsellers as *Lean Forward into Your Life: Begin Each Day As If It Were on Purpose*

Jeanette Rankin (1880–1973): American feminist and politician: first female representative in Congress; elected in Montana, first in 1916, and then again in 1940; first winner of National Organization of Women's Susan B. Anthony Award.

Jacob A. Riis (1849–1914): Danish American "muckraking" journalist and social documentary photographer; best known for his newspaper exposés of slum conditions in New York City; considered one of the fathers of modern photography with his pioneering use of flash photography.

Rainer Maria Rilke (1875–1926): Bohemian Austrian poet and artist whose lyrical and mystical writings in German have been widely translated.

James "Jim" Rogers (1942–): American investor and author; began on his road to wealth at age five selling peanuts and picking up empty bottles; after graduating from both Yale and Oxford, entered into investment banking career, founded Quantum Fund with George Soros; "retired" at age thirty-eight to travel and lecture on finance and investing.

Eleanor Roosevelt (1884–1962): American humanitarian, writer, and, as First Lady, advised her husband, Franklin D. Roosevelt, in political and social affairs, serving as assistant director of civilian defense; later delegate to the UN Assembly and chairperson of the

UN Human Rights Commission; known worldwide for her tireless advocacy of humanitarian causes.

Franklin D. Roosevelt (1882–1945): American politician; 32nd president of the United States; considered one of the most influential U.S. presidents for his New Deal policies during the Great Depression; mobilized the United States against Fascism during World War II; the only president to have served more than two terms.

Theodore Roosevelt (1858–1919): American politician; 26th president of the United States; served as governor of New York; known for his energetic and vigorous personality; besides his work in politics, wrote numerous books, sponsored and participated in scientific expeditions, hunted, and soldiered.

Rumi (Jalal ad-Din Muhammad Balkhi) (1207–1273): Persian poet; one of the most influential Sufi writers and leaders; known for his mystic verses; founded Mewlewi Sufi order; his mystic poems, originally written in Persian, have been translated into numerous languages; he was declared America's most popular poet in 2007.

Alfred Damon Runyon (1880–1946): American writer and newsman; best known for his tales of Broadway tough guys, gamblers, gangsters, and showgirls—later adapted into the musical *Guys and Dolls*.

Salman Rushdie (1947–): British Indian novelist; known for novels, which combine history with magical realism, generally set in India; his book *The Satanic Verses* provoked much controversy and death threats, forcing the author to go into hiding.

George Herman "Babe" Ruth (1895–1948): American baseball player; began as a pitcher, but achieved fame as a home run slugger; arguably the best player in baseball history; known as "the Bambino" and "the Sultan of Swat."

Carl Sandburg (1878–1967): American writer; famed for his Pulitzer Prize–winning poetry and biography of Abraham Lincoln; deemed a quintessentially American writer; especially famous for his beautifully evocative description of Chicago: "Hog Butcher for the World/ Tool Maker, Stacker of Wheat/Player with Railroads and the Nation's Freight Handler/Stormy, Husky, Brawling/ City of the Big Shoulders."

Santigold (Santi White) (1976–): American singer, songwriter, and producer; described by the *New York Times* as being one "of a new crop of young, multicultural, female acts in the wake of M.I.A. causing a stir on the Internet and in indie-label conference rooms"; most recent album is the bestselling *Master of My Make-Believe.*

Adam Savage (1967–): American industrial design and special effects artist, cohost of two Discovery Channel series, *Mythbusters* and *Unchained Reaction*; his models have appeared in the *Star Wars* and *Matrix* films.

Paula Scher (1948–): American graphic designer, educator, and painter; first female principal at famous design studio Pentragram.

Charles M. Schwab (1862–1939): American businessman; an important steel industry entrepreneur who served as president of Carnegie Steel and U.S. Steel; later made Bethlehem Steel the second-largest steel corporation in the United States and a world leader in heavy manufacturing. A big spender, after the Great Depression he was forced to live in a small apartment; he died $300,000 in debt.

Maurice Sendak (1928–2012): American writer and illustrator; beloved for his whimsical yet insightful children's works such as *Where the Wild Things Are.*

William Shatner (1931–): Canadian actor; best known as Captain Kirk in the hit television and film series *Star Trek*; numerous other television and film roles, coauthor of the *TekWar* science-fiction series.

Artie Shaw (Arthur Jacob Arshawsky) (1910–2004): American jazz musician, composer, and writer; widely regarded as jazz's best clarinetist; a popular and innovative big band leader who fused jazz with classical music; his band's signature song, Cole Porter's "Begin the Beguine," was one of the most popular recordings of the big band era.

George Bernard Shaw (1856–1950): Irish writer and critic; cofounder of the London School of Economics; renowned for his numerous plays, often with social commentary and a comedic tone, notably *Pygmalion, Man and Superman,* and *Arms and the Man.* The only person to have won both a Nobel Prize for Literature and an Academy Award.

Sidney Sheldon (Sidney Schechtel) (1917–2007): American writer; began as a stage and screenwriter; won the Academy Award for the classic film *The Bachelor and the Bobby-Soxer;* moved on to television, creating the popular *Patty Duke Show* and *I Dream of Jeannie;* in his fifties began writing novels and became the seventh-bestselling fiction writer of all time.

Neil Simon (1927–): American playwright and screenwriter; author of over 60 plays and screenplays, including the hits *Barefoot in the Park, The Odd Couple, Biloxi Blues, Goodbye Girl,* and *Lost in Yonkers;* has won numerous awards, including Emmys, Tonys, Golden Globes, and the Pulitzer Prize.

Amarillo Slim (Thomas Austin Preston Jr.) (1928–2012): American professional gambler; one of the most famous poker tournament players in the world; winner of the 1972 World Series of Poker; inducted into the Poker Hall of Fame.

Patti Smith (1946–): American singer/songwriter, poet, artist, and activist; her debut album in 1975, *Horses*, helped define punk rock; for this and other albums now known as the "Godmother of Punk"; best known for the song "Because the Night," which was cowritten with Bruce Springsteen and reached number 13 on *Billboard's* Hot 100 chart; winner of the National Book Award for her memoir *Just Kids*.

Willard "Will" Smith (1968–): American actor, producer, and rapper; began career as a rapper named Fresh Prince; gained popularity as the star of the television sitcom *The Fresh Prince of Bel-Air*, then moved into starring roles in numerous blockbuster films, including *Men in Black* and *Independence Day*; called one of the most powerful men in Hollywood.

Aaron Sorkin (1961–): American screenwriter, playwright, and producer; best known for his highly popular Emmy Award–winning TV series about the White House, *The West Wing*, as well as movies like *A Few Good Men* (and its iconic "You can't handle the truth!" line), *The Social Network* (for which he won an Academy Award), and *Moneyball*; his writing is characterized by fast dialogue and extended monologues.

Roger Staubach (1942–): American football player; NFL quarterback who started for the Dallas Cowboys in four Super Bowls, leading them to victory in Super Bowl VI and Super Bowl XII; later founded an extremely successful multibillion-dollar real estate business.

Claude M. Steele (1946–): American social psychologist, professor, and dean at Stanford University; best known for his research in self-image and self-affirmation as well as self-regulation in addictive behaviors.

Benjamin "Ben" Stein (1944–): American actor, writer, lawyer, and political speechwriter and strategist; speechwriter for Presidents Nixon and Ford; later became actor and Emmy Award–winning game show host.

Gertrude Stein (1874–1946): American writer and critic; influenced contemporary artists; applied theories of abstract art to writing. Maintained an unofficial salon for American expatriate writers and artists like Ernest Hemingway and F. Scott Fitzgerald at her Left Bank apartment in Paris.

Casey Stengel (1889–1975): American baseball player and manager; played with the Brooklyn Dodgers; from 1932 as New York Yankees manager led the team to seven World Series victories, later managed the New York Mets; famous for his colorful and unique way of speaking.

Jon Stewart (Jonathan Stuart Leibowitz) (1962–): American political satirist, writer, director, actor, and television host; began his career as a stand-up comedian, then became host for several shows on MTV and Comedy Central; gained fame as host of the *The Daily Show* on Comedy Central, where he pokes fun at mainstream news media and politicians from his fake news desk.

Corey Stoll (1976–): American stage and screen actor; best known for his roles in the play *Intimate Apparel,* for which he received a Drama Desk Award, and on the television show *Law & Order: LA.*

Martha Sturdy: Canadian artist/designer; taking her inspiration from nature, she designs bold and unique jewelry and fashion accessories in resin and metals, as well as furniture, large sculptures, and wall art.

Jeffrey Tambor (1944–): American actor; best known for his quirky supporting roles on television and film, such as Hank Kingsley on *The Larry Sanders Show* and George Bluth Sr. and Oscar Bluth on *Arrested Development.*

Mother Teresa (Agnes Gonxha Bojaxhiu) (1910–1997): Catholic nun and missionary; born to Albanian parents in what is today Macedonia; became a Catholic sister at age twelve; taught in India for seventeen years before she experienced her "call within a call" to care for the sick and poor; founded the Missionaries of Charity;

established a hospice and centers for the dying and disabled; received the Nobel Peace Prize in 1979; was beatified by the Catholic Church in 2003.

Twyla Tharp (1941–): American dancer and choreographer; founder of the world-acclaimed dance company Twyla Tharp Dance; worked with Mikhail Baryshnikov at the American Ballet Theatre; choreographed numerous award-winning shows like *Movin' Out*; brought to Broadway her *The Times They Are A-Changin',* inspired by Bob Dylan's music.

Usher (Usher Terry Raymond IV) (1978–): American R&B singer, songwriter, and actor; began singing professionally at age eleven; now one of the bestselling entertainers in music history, having sold 65 million records worldwide; became a coach on TV talent show *The Voice* in 2013.

Michael Uslan (1952–): American film producer; known chiefly as the producer of the highly successful *Batman* movies; first instructor to ever teach an accredited college-level course on comic books, The Comic Book in Society, which led to major press coverage, the attention of comic book master Stan Lee and DC Comics, and ultimately his high-profile film series.

Vincent van Gogh (1853–1890): Dutch artist; self-taught post-Impressionist painter whose bold, colorful, emotional paintings had an enormous impact on

20th-century art; considered the greatest Dutch painter, along with Rembrandt; sadly, virtually unknown during his lifetime; sold only one painting; committed suicide in despair.

Meredith Vieira (1953–): American journalist and television personality; original moderator for ABC's show *The View* and cohost of NBC's morning news show *Today*; former host of the game show *Who Wants to Be a Millionaire*; contributor to *Dateline NBC*.

Kurt Vonnegut Jr. (1922–2007): American writer; famed for satirical novels that often include elements of science-fiction and fantasy, most notably *Slaughterhouse-Five*; in later life became an elder statesman of American literature and a fervent opponent of militarism and censorship.

Denis Waitley (1933–): Business development consultant; author of numerous self-help books including *The Psychology of Winning* and *Empires of the Mind*; founding member of the National Council for Self-Esteem; has counseled numerous people, including Apollo astronauts, executives, and returning American POWs.

Jimmy Wales (1966–): American tech entrepreneur; after earning degrees in finance, started a web portal with adult entertainment content in the late 1990s; with others, launched free open-content, peer-reviewed online encyclopedia Wikipedia (dubbed the world's largest encyclopedia) in 2001; since then has become the face of the site and its chief spokesman; he claims he founded it alone, although he is typically dubbed a cofounder.

Denzel Washington (1954–): American actor, film director, and producer, known for numerous powerful acting roles, including his portrayal of historical figures such as Malcolm X, Hurricane Carter, and Steven Biko; star of such major films as *Philadelphia, Pelican Brief,* and *Antwone Fisher*; winner of two Academy Awards.

Kerry Washington (1977–): American actress; star of the hit television drama series *Scandal*; also known for her political activism.

John Waters (1946–): American film director, screenwriter, and actor; began making violent cult films shown to small audiences in his hometown of Baltimore, Maryland; rose to fame with the ultimate bad-taste film *Pink Flamingos*; crossed into the mainstream with *Hairspray*, which nevertheless still shows the odd transgressive Waters's touch.

Emma Watson (1990–): English actress; noted for her portrayal of Hermione Granger in the *Harry Potter* film series.

Bill Watterson (1958–): American cartoonist; best known for his classic *Calvin and Hobbes* comic strip, about an iconoclastic little boy and his stuffed tiger; the cartoon ran from 1985 to 1995, at which point Watterson announced he had done all he could with *Calvin and Hobbes*. Watterson is also well known for refusing to license his characters, feeling it would cheapen them.

Mae West (Mary Jane West) (1893–1980): American actress, playwright, and screenwriter; began as a performer in burlesque and Vaudeville; best known for her spicy film roles (in which she wrote or cowrote her dialogue) marked by witty sexual double entendres, such as *I'm No Angel* and *She Done Him Wrong*.

Joseph Hill "Joss" Whedon (1964–): American producer, screenwriter, and comic book author; creator of the popular and critically acclaimed *Buffy the Vampire Slayer* TV series; writer and producer of the hit movie *The Avengers* and its sequel.

Kristen Wiig (1973–): American comedian and actress; best known for her work as a member of the *Saturday Night Live* comedy series from 2005 to 2012; also starred in and cowrote the hit film *Bridesmaids*.

Serena Williams (1981–): American tennis player; regarded as one of the greatest tennis players of all time; ranked number-one women's singles tennis player six times, and in 2013 became the oldest number-one player in World Tennis Association history.

Theodore "Ted" Williams (1918–2002): American baseball player and manager; played his entire career for the Boston Red Sox; nicknamed "The Splendid Splinter" for his batting prowess; the last player to bat over .400 for a single season.

Venus Williams (1980–): American tennis player; ranked number-one female singles player by the World Tennis Association three different times; won seven Grand Slam singles titles, twenty-two overall.

Bruce Willis (1955–): American actor and producer; gained fame for his role as wisecracking detective David Addison opposite Cybill Shepard in TV show *Moonlighting*; has gone on to be one of the most successful leading men in Hollywood, making over sixty films; perhaps best known for his lead role in the *Die Hard* film series.

Oprah Winfrey (1954–): American talk show host, actress, entrepreneur, and philanthropist; born in poverty in rural Mississippi; rose to become the world's richest woman; hosted the highest-rated talk show in television history; has won numerous Emmys; credited with reviving interest in reading by featuring selected books on her show and in her magazine, *O*.

Jonathan Winters (1925–2013): American comedian, actor, writer, and artist; a pioneer in stand-up improvisational comedy; a master of mimicry, dialects, and sound effects; winner of numerous awards, including an Emmy; described by television host Jack Paar to be "pound for pound, the funniest man alive."

John Wooden (1910–2010): American basketball player and coach; known as the "Wizard of Westwood" for his role as coach leading the UCLA basketball team to ten NCAA championships in a twelve-year period; known for his inspiring maxims that directed players to success on and off the court.

Frank Zappa (1940–1993): American rock musician and music producer; produced over sixty albums he released with his band The Mothers of Invention and as a solo act; a leading experimental rocker who incorporated diverse elements in his music from classical to R&B to jazz; known for his musical iconoclasm and improvisation, as well as his pointed social commentary; after his death, was made a member of the Rock and Roll Hall of Fame and received a Grammy Lifetime Achievement Award.

ABOUT THE AUTHORS

Kathryn and Ross Petras, sister-and-brother quotations connoisseurs, have published numerous collections of their finds. Kathryn Petras lives in Seattle; Ross Petras lives in Toronto.